CO

WHERE to fish is still top of the pops in what anglers want to know. The survey, in last year's *Annual*, of fisheries controlled by the giant London and Birmingham Anglers' Associations proved very popular.

That is why this year's *Annual* features a major review, including A-to-Z easy-reference guides, of the commercially-operated fisheries run by Leisure Sport and the Redlands/O.W.R. scheme. Their fisheries are chiefly lakes developed from former gravel pits and open to you in return for a modestly-priced annual permit or, in some cases, day tickets.

As in previous years, some of the features in these 96 pages have been selected, adapted or condensed from those previously published in *Angler's Mail* and here worth a more permanent place within a hard-cover book that, I know, thousands have collected since the first *Annual* in 1973.

FINALLY, a personal farewell. By the time this edition reaches you I will have retired from *Angler's Mail* after 20 years as its editor, including 18 as Publisher or General Manager, and close on 40 with the owners of this and a wide range of other household names in the magazine publishing industry.

I have thoroughly enjoyed earning my living from a sport that was a first love in childhood and now look forward to more fishing time than the job actually ever allowed!

JOHN INGHAM

£3.25

What commercial LAKES GALORE!

LAKE fishing is increasingly popular, especially in the main fair-weather months of the season when amateur armadas of holiday boats test angling nerves and patience to the limit on most of the popular navigable rivers and waterways.

The majority of fishing lakes are man-made water-filled holes in the ground left by gravel extraction needed to build runways for wartime airfields and, more recently, for the nation's network of motorways. Many of these gravel pits were once no more than eyesores, often used as village dumps for anything from unwanted mattresses to old bangers.

Bur progressive re-development in the last 15 to 20 years by subsidiary companies formed as offshoots by the giants of the gravel extracting industry, has produced a transformation of considerable benefit to anglers, wildlife conservationists and bird lovers. Not to mention scores of swans, which have fled from boat-ravaged rivers to find peaceful lake sanctuaries for rearing their young.

The biggest group of commercially-operated stillwaters is run by Leisure Sport Angling, which is a member of the Ready Mixed Concrete group, with a total of 105 lakes and 16 stretches of river, or relief channel, under its control.

And the Redlands Angling Scheme, formed by a merger between Redland Ltd., one of the major gravel extractors, and the Outdoor Water Recreation

Compiled by MIKE GUNNELL

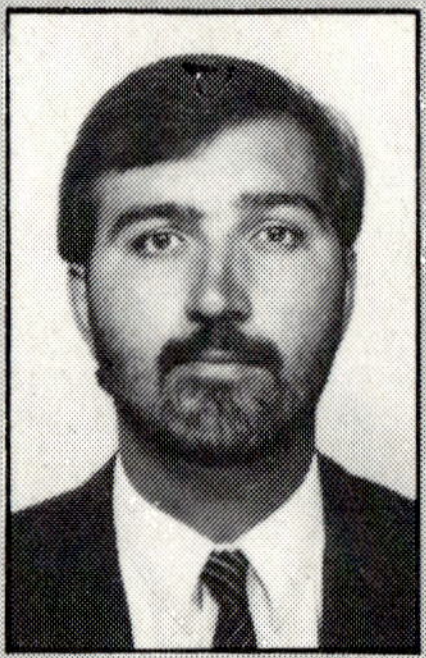

Group, manages 11 fishery complexes comprising 18 lakes and six stretches of river or navigation channel.

Thousands of coarse fishing enthusiasts enjoy the advantages offered by membership of these two schemes and use them for planning annual holiday angling trips or for regular outings — even for matches among themselves.

Angler's Mail Annual commissioned this special survey of both schemes, and prepared a full A-Z guide to all the fisheries involved, as a follow-up to our survey, in the 1986 Annual, of the fisheries managed by the giant London Anglers' Association and Birmingham Anglers' Association. This proved very popular with readers, who clearly want more of the same to help plan where and when to fish.

Remember, as always, that an appropriate Water Authority rod licence is needed, wherever you fish. These are usually available at local tackle shops in the area.

LEISURE SPORT FISHERIES

LEISURE Sport Angling runs the biggest group of commercially-operated stillwater fisheries in the country and one of the largest clubs with more than 14,000 members.

That is why LSA, with waters from Lincolnshire to Hampshire, can claim to offer fishing facilities for a large percentage of the nation's anglers at a reasonable cost.

A total of 105 lakes and 16 stretches of river, or relief channel, means there is something on offer for every kind of angler — and much of the fishing reaches a very high standard.

Leisure Sport's records indicate just how high that quality is:

Species	LSA record	Venue	Year	British official record
Bream	13¼lb.	Yateley	1981	13¾lb.
Carp	45¾lb.	Yateley	1984	44lb.
Crucian carp	4lb. 6oz.	Stanford-le-Hope	1984	5lb. 10½oz.
Dace	1lb. 2oz.	Darenth	1979	1lb. 4¼oz.
Pike	33lb. 6oz.	Attenborough	1984	40lb.
Roach	3lb. 5oz.	Yateley	1980	4lb. 1oz.
Tench	9lb. 12oz.	Wraysbury	1984	12lb. 8oz. 11dms.

Action at Attenborough fishery, LSA's largest complex.

With one fish over the official target and several near-misses, Leisure Sport catches clearly rate among the best in the land.

Leisure Sport is a member of the Ready Mixed Concrete group with origins dating back to the Hall's Angling Scheme which was prominent in the 1960's. A take-over of that scheme by RMC produced Leisure Sport Ltd., which was integrated to form the present Leisure Sport Angling.

Manager Jack Ashford is dedicated to continued improvement and upgrading. The latest move in this direction is the acquisition, in March 1986, of the 200-acre Hykeham Gravels, near Lincoln, as this edition of *Angler's Mail Annual* went to press.

The majority of LSA venues are available only on a season ticket basis; a limited number can be fished on a day ticket. But from the highest charge of £30 a year for Darenth lakes in Kent, — rated one of the South's finest carp fisheries — to the lowest of £10 for a full year's fishing, the season tickets are well within the reach of most anglers and represent excellent value.

Once you join Leisure Sport you can take advantage of a number of members-only offers, including tackle prizes for the best fish caught, discounts for introducing new members and reduced entry charges to Thorpe Pleasure Park with its many rides, attractions and shows.

For the junior anglers LSA offer the Striker Club for those aged 17 or under, with tackle prizes for "Striker of the Month" and a weekly Lucky Striker draw.

Full details of all venues and charges are obtainable from LSA, Thorpe Park, Staines Road, Chertsey, Surrey KT16 8PN.

SEASON PERMITS ONLY

Attenborough North

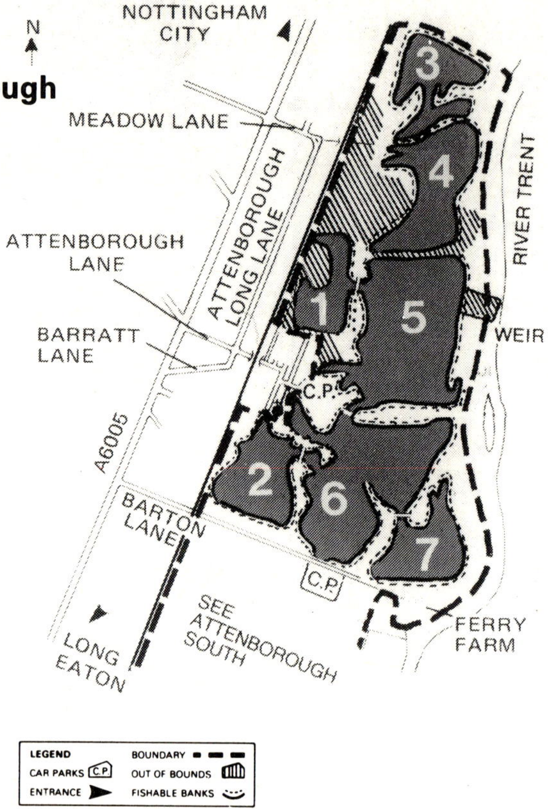

ATTENBOROUGH FISHERY

ATTENBOROUGH Fishery, near Nottingham, is Leisure Sport's largest with a complex of 10 lakes and two stretches of the River Trent covering over 420 acres of water.

Split into two halves, Attenborough North and Attenborough South, the fishery is noted for the quality of its sport for most species. The lakes offer carp, bream, roach, tench and crucians, plus pike to 27½lb. The River Trent, rated by many as the best in the country, offers barbel, carp, chub, roach and bream and some excellent mixed bags have been recorded.

Fishing in the Attenborough North section is by season permit only and matches are held on the famous Attenborough Gravels lake for LSA members exclusively. Over the years these events have produced many excellent bags of bream with fish to over 7lb landed. The match water is Lake Seven and non-match members should note that they may not be able to fish here when contests are taking place.

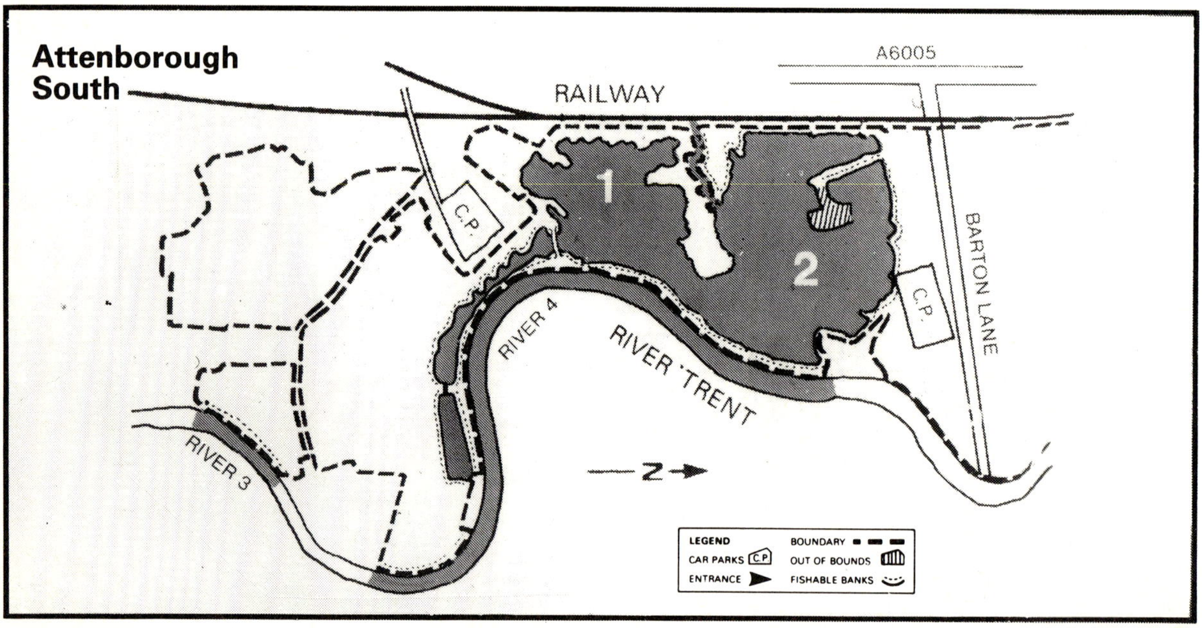

Day tickets are available at Attenborough South section from: Gordon Plummer, 45 Beresford Road, Sawley, Long Eaton, Nottingham, tel: Long Eaton 3245 (who also takes bookings for matches on the River Trent) and Frank Russell, "Wotsits" Tackle Shop, Archer Road, Staplesford, Notts, tel: Nottingham 396096, who also handles bookings for matches (100 pegs) for the north end of Lake Two. Day tickets may also be purchased from bailiffs on the banks.

No night fishing is allowed at Attenborough North or South; fishing is from dawn to dusk only.

Attenborough North is situated in Long Lane, a short distance from Attenborough British Rail station and just off the A6005. Attenborough South lies off Barton Lane, which runs between the two fisheries.

Wraysbury No. 1 lake, which produced Leisure Sport's record tench of 9¾lb.

WRAYSBURY LAKES

THE Wraysbury venue near Staines, in Middlesex, contains two lakes totalling some 138 acres, one of the largest that LSA offers.

These lakes have a reputation for being "difficult" at times, but both are stocked with some fish of exceptional size. Andrew McRae, of Reading, set a new LSA tench record when he landed a 9¾lb specimen from this fishery, in 1984.

Carp to 38¼lb, pike to 27¼lb, bream to 10lb 2oz and roach to 3lb 6oz have all been taken from the same No. 1 lake.

Lake Two should not be discounted, however, as it has produced notable fish, including pike to 28lb 6oz, bream to 7lb, tench to 7lb 3oz and roach over 3lb.

Wraysbury is a single permit water or may be fished on a group permit. Day tickets are also issued, in advance, from Wraysbury Newsagents in Wraysbury High Street or Davies Angling, Church Street, Staines.

The venue is shared with Kingmead Fish Farms and members are warned that trout pens may be moored at any point in the lake. Fishing within casting distance of the pens is strictly forbidden.

The lakes lie within half-an-hour of central London, just off the A30 main road, and outside the village of Wraysbury itself, which has a direct rail service from Waterloo (SR) to Wraysbury and Sunnymeads stations on the Windsor line.

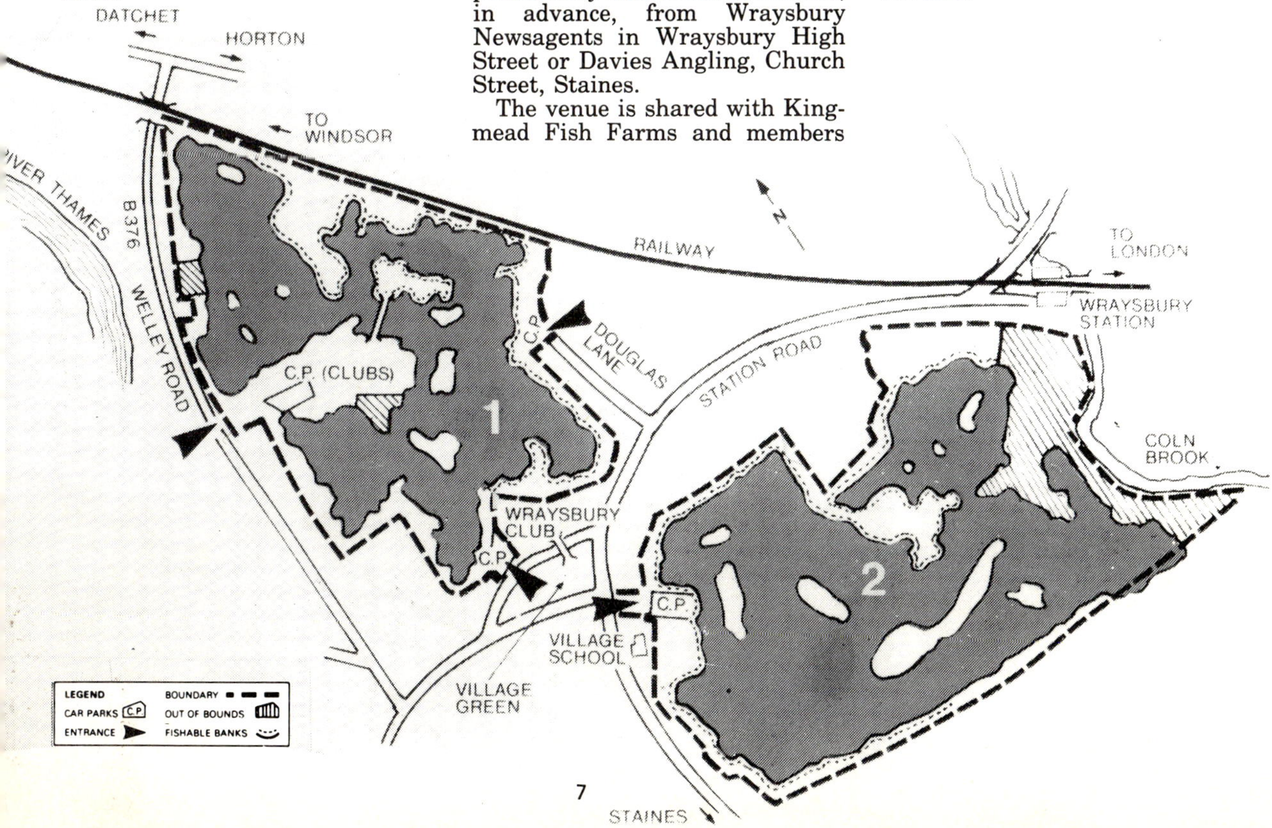

YATELEY LAKES

THE Yateley complex of lakes, near Camberley, Surrey, is Leisure Sport's pride and joy and must rate as one of the most consistent producers of big fish in the country.

No less than five LSA records have come from this one fishery, including a 45½lb carp, a 13¼lb bream and a 3lb 5oz roach.

With 14 lakes to choose from a visitor is almost spoilt for choice as the majority contain big fish and are each worth a go in their own right.

The complex is split in two by the Sandhurst Road. Those waters to the west of the road, known as Yateley West, are well established, well weeded and hold big tench, carp, bream and pike.

It was from one of these waters that Ritchie McDonald of Richmond, Surrey, caught a 45¾lb carp in the summer of 1984. Although the fish beat the official British record of 44lb, Ritchie declined to claim his fish as a record as he believed a 51½lb carp, caught by Chris Yates in 1980, to be the true record.

Lakes Two and Three hold a large head of sizeable roach, rudd and tench and give excellent sport for the pleasure angler. The other lakes are generally more rewarding for serious, big-fish anglers.

East Yateley lakes to the east of Sandhurst Road, also hold large specimens. Carp to 38lb, bream to 12½lb, tench to over 8lb and pike to 30lb have all been taken here.

Lake 11 is designated the "match lake" where occasional matches are held at weekends and mid-week evenings. Permit holders are advised to check on availability with the LSA centre at Chertsey, especially at weekends.

Due to its popularity, Yateley has been designated a Special Venue with only a limited number of season permits issued each season to prevent overcrowding.

Location — within an hour's drive of central London, just off the busy A30 road. Night fishing allowed but camping, bright lights and radios are forbidden.

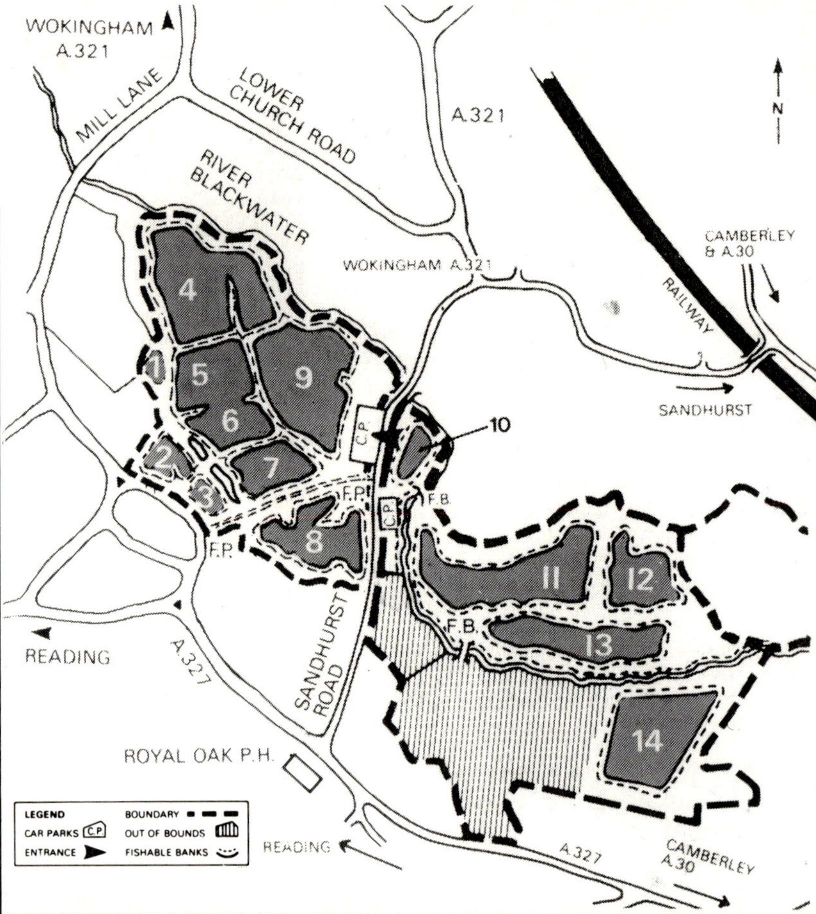

One of the 14 lakes in the Yateley complex.

A-Z GUIDE TO LEISURE SPORT VENUES

THE following group of 21 fisheries are available by purchasing a permit for a single fishery or a group water permit which gives access to them all.

ASH VALE LAKES, Ash Vale, Surrey. Three lakes, comprising 12 acres, stocked with carp, crucians, tench, roach, rudd, perch and pike. Night fishing allowed.

Season ticket £12 for adults, £6 juniors, OAP's and disabled anglers. No day tickets.

ATTENBOROUGH LAKES, near Nottingham. Attenborough North, Attenborough, Beeston, Notts: Seven lakes comprising 181 acres. Stocked with bream, perch, carp, roach, tench, crucians, plus large pike, best 33lb 6oz.

No day tickets. Season tickets £14 adults, £7 juniors, OAPs and disabled.

Matches held on Sundays and Wednesdays for members only. Organiser, S. Toone, 42 Devon Drive, Ruddington, Notts. Matches held on Lake No. 7.

No night fishing, fishing from dawn to dusk only.

Attenborough South, Long Eaton, nr Nottingham. Two lakes totalling 142 acres. Two stretches of the River Trent comprising 2,500 metres. Lakes contain bream, roach and pike. Chub, roach, barbel, carp and bream from the river.

This is a combined season permit and day-ticket fishery. Season tickets are £14 for adults and £7 for juniors, OAPs and disabled. Day tickets £1.20, available from Frank Russell, "Wotsits" Tackle Shop, 8 Archer Road, Stapleford, Notts. Weekend matches on the River Trent and on the north end of Lake No. 2 can be booked in advance.

BROXBOURNE LAKES, nr Broxbourne, Hoddesdon, Herts. Four lakes totalling 125 acres, stocked with pike, carp, tench, chub, bream, roach, crucians, perch and eels.

Season permits £14 adults, £7 juniors, OAPs and disabled. No day tickets. Night fishing allowed.

BURGHFIELD FISHERY, Pingewood, nr Burghfield, Berkshire. Three lakes totalling 100 acres plus 1,300 metre stretch of River Kennet. Lakes stocked with bream, tench, carp, golden orfe and pike. Barbel, chub, roach, perch and eels from the river.

Season tickets £17 adults, £8.50 juniors, OAPs and disabled. No day tickets. Night fishing allowed.

CHERTSEY FISHERY, Thorpe Road, nr Chertsey, Surrey. Lake of 4.25 acres, plus 1,000 metres of River Bourne. Bream, perch, pike, roach and carp in the lake. Chub, roach and gudgeon from Bourne.

Season tickets £13 adults, £6.50 juniors, OAPs and disabled. No day tickets. Night fishing not allowed. No access to Thorpe Park via culvert under M3 is allowed.

CHIGBOROUGH LAKES, Scraley Road, Maldon, Essex. Two lakes totalling 8½ acres, stocked with perch, roach, tench, bream and eels. Some flounders from Lake 2.

Season permits £12 adults, £6 juniors, OAPS and disabled. Night fishing allowed.

FRIMLEY LAKES, Frimley, Farnborough, Hants. Ten lakes totalling 37 acres, plus short stretch of River Blackwater. Stocks include bream, tench to 7lb, roach to 2½lb, perch, crucians, pike and carp to over 25lb.

Season permits £15 adults, £7.50 juniors, OAPs and disabled.

LARKFIELD LAKES, Lunsford Lane, Larkfield, nr Maidstone, Kent. Three lakes comprising 91 acres, stocked with carp to 28lb, bream to 10lb, tench to 8½lb, eels, roach, perch and pike to 27lb. Night fishing allowed.

Season permits £14 and £7 respectively. No day tickets.

LEIGHTON BUZZARD LAKES, Heath and Reach, nr Leighton Buzzard, Beds. Two lakes totalling 11 acres, stocked with pike, carp, tench, roach and bream; also holds catfish — the best of 23¼lb set a new LSA record.

Season tickets £12 and £6. No day tickets. Night fishing allowed.

NEWDIGATE LAKES, New Barn Lane, Newdigate, nr Dorking, Surrey. Two lakes totalling 12 acres, stocked mainly with carp to 8lb. Season permits £12 and £6. No day tickets. Night fishing allowed.

RIVER GIPPING, Bramford, nr Ipswich, Suffolk. Stretch of river, 1,050 metres long, stocked with roach, small bream and eels. Season permits £10 and £5. No day tickets. Night fishing allowed.

RIVER WEY, Wey Manor, Addlestone, Surrey. Two stretches of river totalling 525 metres stocked with chub, roach, dace and pike, plus occasional barbel and wild carp.

Season permits £11 and £5.50. No day tickets. Night fishing allowed.

RIVERS OUSE AND IVEL, Harold and Biggleswade, Beds. Stretch of River Ouse, 1,050 metres, stocked with bream, chub, roach and dace. Stretch of River Ivel, 1,200 metres, holding dace, chub, roach, barbel, carp and trout.

Season permits £10 and £5 to cover both venues. No day tickets. Night fishing allowed.

RYEMEADS LAKES, Toll Road, Rye House, Roydon, Herts. Two lakes totalling 16½ acres, stocked with pike to 22lb, tench to 7lb, bream to 9lb, chub to 5¼lb.

Season permits £13 and £6.50. No day tickets. Night fishing allowed.

SHEPPERTON LAKES, Penny Lane, Walton Bridge, Shepperton, Middlesex. Two lakes totalling 15½ acres, containing wild carp, roach to 2½lb, perch, eels, pike to 25lb, bream and tench.

Season permits £13 and £6.50. No day tickets. No night fishing (dawn to dusk only).

STANFORD-LE-HOPE LAKES, Wharf Road, Stanford-Le-Hope, Essex. Two lakes totalling 13 acres, stocked with pike, carp, perch, roach, eels, bream, tench, rudd and crucians.

Season permits cost £14 and £7. No day tickets. Night fishing allowed.

STANSTEAD ABBOTS, Marsh Lane, Stanstead Abbots, Herts. Five lakes totalling 40 acres, plus 6,990 metres of River Lea and Mill Stream. Lakes stocked with tench to 7lb, roach, carp to over 30lb, crucians, bream and large pike. Barbel, chub, pike, roach, dace, bream and perch have been taken from Lea and Mill Stream.

Season permits £16 and £8. No day tickets. Night fishing allowed.

TAVERHAM FISHERY, Old Costessey, nr Norwich, Norfolk. Seven lakes totalling 12 acres, plus 480 metres of River Wensum. Bream to 6½lb, tench, roach, common carp and crucians from lake. Chub, dace and roach from river.

Season permits £12 and £3. Day tickets (in advance) cost £1.20 and 60p from Huntsman Motor Caravanette Centre and Filling Station, Old Costessey. Penalty tickets, £1.40 and 70p, issued on the bank.

THEALE LAKES, Station Road, Theale, nr Reading, Berks. Two lakes totalling 52 acres, containing bream, tench, pike and roach. Season permits £14 and £7. No day tickets or night fishing.

TWYFORD CHARVIL AND ST. PATRICK'S STREAM, Twyford, nr Reading, Berks. Two lakes totalling 45 acres; 565 metre stretch of River Loddon and 1,420 metres of St. Patrick's Stream. Tench, pike, roach, perch, eels, bream and carp from lakes. Chub, barbel, roach and dace from Loddon. St. Patrick's Stream noted for barbel which must not be retained in keepnets, chub and roach. Season permits £14 and £7. Night fishing allowed. No day tickets.

WRAYSBURY LAKES, Wraysbury, nr Staines, Middlesex. Two lakes totalling 138 acres, containing carp to 38lb, pike to 27lb, double-figure bream, tench, roach to 3lb 6oz, perch and eels.

Season permits £14 and £7. Day tickets available in advance from Davies Angling, 47 Church Street, Staines; Wraysbury Newsagents, Wraysbury High Street or Leisure Sport headquarters at Thorpe Park. Night fishing allowed.

● **All 21 venues available on a group water permit costing £29 for adults and £14.50 for juniors, OAPs and disabled, giving access to a total of 65 lakes and 15 stretches of river.**

SPECIAL VENUES

Leisure Sport Angling also control 10 single-water fisheries which are designated as "Special Venues" where a strict limit is imposed on the number of permits issued. Some of these require the permit holder to be issued with a key to provide access (£2 deposit for each key).

Renewal of permits for "Special Venues" is offered to existing permit holders first; any permits not renewed then become available on a first-come first-served basis.

Venues which have already filled their allocation of permit holders are indicated on the application form but LSA do operate a waiting list at their Thorpe Park HQ. For full details and application forms contact LSA at Thorpe Park, Staines Lane, Chertsey, Surrey KT16 8PN.

ALDERMASTON, Paices Hill, Aldermaston, nr Reading, Berks. Eight lakes totalling nearly 10 acres, stocked with carp, perch, tench, rudd and bream. Season tickets £17 adults, £9 juniors, OAPs and disabled. No key required. Night fishing allowed.

AMWELL, High Street, Stanstead Abbots, nr Ware, Herts. Two lakes totalling nearly nine acres, stocked with tench, bream, roach, plus carp, best reported at 31lb.

Season ticket £14 and £9 respectively. No key required. Night fishing allowed.

BOREHAM, Wallace's Farm, Russell Green, Little Waltham, nr Chelmsford, Essex. One lake of 1¼ acres, stocked with bream, tench, carp, pike and roach.

Season permits £14 and £7 respectively. No night fishing allowed. No key required.

DARENTH, Parsonage Lane, Darenth, nr Dartford, Kent. Five lakes totalling 30 acres rated as one of the best carp fisheries in Kent. Best fish reported at 32¼lb, many over 20lb. Other stocks include pike (best 31½lb), bream, tench, perch, roach, rudd and chub.

Season permits £30 and £21 respectively. Night fishing allowed. Key required for access. No prebaiting. Two rods only.

FISHERS GREEN, Waltham Abbey, Esssex. Two lakes totalling 133 acres; 3,900 metre stretch of Old River Lea and 3,100 metre stretch of Lea Relief Channel. The lakes contain pike, tench, bream and roach, barbel, chub, perch, bream, plus roach in the river and channel.

Season permits £23 and £16 respectively. No night fishing. Key required for access. Barbel not to be kept in nets. No tins or bottles to be taken on to venue.

PAPERCOURT, Send Marsh, Papercourt, nr Ripley, Surrey. Lake of 32 acres, stocked with pike, carp, bream, tench, chub, perch, roach, rudd and eels, all to specimen size. Night fishing allowed. Key required for access.

Season permits £17 and £9 respectively.

RICKMANSWORTH, Tolpits Lane, Rickmansworth, Herts. Two lakes totalling over seven acres, plus 600 metre stretch of River Colne. Carp, pike, tench, bream, chub, roach and perch from river.

Season permits £16 and £8 respectively. Night fishing allowed. Key required for access.

STAINES, Staines Road, Wraysbury, nr Staines, Middlesex. Three lakes totalling seven acres, stocked with carp, bream, tench, roach, crucian, pike, and perch all to specimen size.

Season permits £17 and £9 respectively. Night fishing allowed. Key required for access.

SUTTON-AT-HONE, Devon Road, Sutton-at-Hone, nr Dartford, Kent. Three lakes totalling nine acres, stocked with tench, carp, chub, pike, perch, bream, roach and eels.

Season permits £16 and £9 respectively. No night fishing. No key required for access.

YATELEY, Sandhurst Road, Yateley, nr Camberley, Surrey. Fourteen lakes totalling 86 acres, plus short stretch of River Blackwater. The lakes have produced carp to 45¾lb, bream to 13¼lb, pike to 30lb and tench to 9lb; also contains roach, rudd and crucians. River holds small roach, dace, chub and occasional trout.

Season permits £20 and £10 respectively. Night fishing allowed. No key required for access.

DAY TICKETS: The LSA has one fishery that is available on day ticket only. This is **HOOKS MARSH, Fishers Green, Farm Road, Waltham Abbey, Essex,** a 40-acre lake stocked with bream, tench, roach, perch and pike.

Day tickets £1.20 and 60p available from P&B Hall, 44 Highbridge Street, Waltham Abbey and Mick's Tackle Shop, 1A High Street, Harlow or from bailiffs on the bank at penalty rate of £1.40 and 70p respectively.

● **In addition to permits already mentioned, LSA also offer a limited number of Coverall Permits which allow a holder to fish all 31 venues. If purchased separately, permits to fish these waters would cost £213 but a Coverall Permit is offered at £120 for adults and £60 for juniors, OAPs and disabled. As five of the venues require keys for access an additional deposit of £10 is also required.**

Application forms for Single Water Permits, Group Permits, Special Venue Permits and Coverall Permits are available from LSA, Thorpe Park, Staines Lane, Chertsey, Surrey. Tel. Chertsey 64872 for further details.

OWR

REDLAND FISHERIES

Old Bury Hill lake, near Dorking, Surrey, is the flagship of Redland's group of fisheries.

A QUARTER of a million satisfied customers every year is the proud boast of the OWR/Redland Angling Scheme, managed by Graham Rowles.

That figure is only an estimate but Graham is confident that it represents the number of visits to Redland's Fisheries by season ticket and day-ticket anglers during a single year.

Redland's policy is simple and definite — day tickets available at all their 11 fishery complexes, comprising 18 lakes and six stretches of river or navigation channel.

Season tickets are also available for each fishery but it is the intention of Redland's directors to offer good fishing at a "sampling" price well within the reach of any angler, who can then go for a season ticket facility after getting a feel for the water and wanting more of the same.

The majority of Redland's waters are centred around London and the Home Counties, in an intended plan to surround the capital and its environs with high quality, public fisheries.

Redland's Angling Scheme came about in the mid and late 1970's when the directors of Redland Ltd, a major gravel working company, approached Graham Rowles, then manager of the Outdoor Water Recreation Group (OWR).

The result was a merger of the two to form the present company with Graham Rowles at its head and directing operations from his home by the side of Old Bury Hill lake, near Dorking, Surrey.

Resident or local managers are a feature of all Redland's fisheries to add to the personal touch which the company tries to encourage at all their venues.

OLD BURY HILL LAKE

VIEWED as the "flagship" of the Redland's group of water, Old Bury Hill lake near Dorking, in Surrey, has something on offer for everyone.

For specialist anglers there are zander — an unusual stock for a stillwater but which have taken well with fish approaching 20lb, well over the British record, now thought to be in residence. Specimens over 14lb have been taken and many anglers believe it is only a question of time before the "big one" comes out.

For general fishing, Old Bury Hill has much to recommend it, with several of the 100 swims capable of producing large hauls of good-sized bream and tench.

It is also an excellent water for a newcomer to angling, with comfortable banks, a good depth of water close in, and plenty of roach, rudd and perch to keep a float dipping under.

Boats are available to tackle more inaccessible spots. Toilets and a small refreshment hut add to the comforts.

Old Bury Hill lake is just off the A25 Dorking to Guildford road and less than a mile from the town of Dorking. There are frequent train and Green Line coach services from London to Dorking North and from this station the lake is only a short bus journey via Nos. 412 and 773 to Milton Street, Westcott.

First time visitors should note that keepnets are banned in the interests of fish stocks.

SAVAY LAKE

SAVAY Lake near Denham, in Buckinghamshire has the reputation of one of the premier carp fisheries in the country and lies only 20 miles from the heart of London.

This location makes it an extremely popular venue with anglers from London area and pressure on swims, particularly at the start of the season, can be considerable.

But despite this, Savay continues to produce specimen-sized carp with several in excess of 30lb taken every year, along with dozens of 20 pounders.

Big tench, bream and pike have also been netted and roach and perch over 2lb are a common sight at Savay.

Almost half of the lake is open to the public, providing well over 100 comfortable bank swims in very pleasant surroundings.

Savay is best approached from the A40 Oxford road, turning right into the A412 North Orbital Road, once in Denham. After roughly ½ mile, turn right into Moorfield Road, just past Denham railway station. The entrance to the lake is a further 800 yards on the right.

Savay Lake offers excellent fishing for most species, in pleasant surroundings just 20 miles from the centre of London.

There are excellent public transport services. No 347 bus passes by the entrance and Denham railway station on the Marylebone-Banbury line is less than half a mile away.

A-Z GUIDE TO OWR/REDLAND VENUES

Day or Season Tickets available for each fishery

CROWN FISHERY, Broxbourne, Herts.
Three lakes totalling 40 acres, plus one mile of River Lea and ¾-mile of Lea Navigation Channel. Tench, bream and pike in the lakes; roach, chub and barbel in river and channel.

Lakes and River Lea may be fished only by season ticket holders. Cost £12 adults, £6 juniors and OAPs. Lea Navigation may be fished on £1 day ticket, 50p juniors and OAPs.

FARTHINGS LAKE, Battle, nr Hastings, Sussex.
Four-acre lake, set in beautiful wooded valley, and holds carp, tench, bream, roach and rudd.

Season tickets £20 adults, £11.50 juniors and OAPs. Limited number of day tickets at £2 for adults, £1.25 for juniors, OAPs and evenings. **These must be obtained before fishing.** Season tickets from 6, Warwick Road, Bexhill-on-Sea, East Sussex, tel: 0424 224908. Day tickets from Stiles Garage or Surridge Newsagents, Battle High Street, or on 0424 224908.

HOLLYBUSH LANE LAKES, Farnborough, Hants.
Three lakes totalling 20 acres, mainly bream, reach and tench but with some specimen carp and pike.

Day tickets £1 for adults, 50p juniors, OAPs and evenings, available for **car park lake only** and must be obtained before commencing to fish from J & A Newsagents, 201 Lynchford Road (300 yards from fishery, open daily).

Season tickets £12 and £6 respectively available for car park lake and the large lake but NOT for the carp lake in between. Contact Redlands manager Graham Rowles, Lakeview Farm, Old Bury Hill, Dorking, Surrey, tel: Dorking 883621.

The carp lake may be fished only by holders of the special carp season ticket for which there are no vacancies, at present.

HOLWELL HYDE LAKE, Welwyn Garden City, Herts.
Two-acre lake stocked with carp, tench, roach, rudd and perch.

Season tickets £15 adults, £10 juniors, OAPs, and evenings. Day tickets £2 and £1 respectively. Open from sunrise to sunset for season and advance day-ticket holders. Non-ticket holders not allowed on fishery until 8.30am. Bailiff comes round. No night fishing.

Season and advance day tickets from V. Bamford, Holwell Hyde Cottage, Holwell Hyde Lane, Welwyn Garden City, Herts.

KINGS WEIR FISHERY, Wormley, Herts.
Twenty-acre lake, ½-mile of old River Lea, including weirpool, and ¾-mile of Flood Relief Channel. Bream, tench and pike from lake and channel, barbel, chub and roach from river. The river may be fished by season ticket holders only, cost £20 adults, £10 juniors and OAPs. One guest ticket a day per member allowed, booked in advance, £2.

Day tickets £1 adults, 50p juniors and OAPs, available on bank of both lake and Flood Relief Channel. Season tickets for both cost £10 and £5, respectively.

Weirpool maybe fished from punts, bookable in advance at £5 a day.

Details of all tickets from W.E Newton, Kings Weir Fishery, Wormley, Herts, tel: Hoddesdon 468394.

LITTLE PAXTON FISHERY, St Neots, Hunts.
Three lakes totalling 20 acres, plus ½-mile of Great Ouse. Bream, roach, tench, carp and pike in lakes, roach and chub in river. Season tickets £10 adults, £5 juniors and OAPs. Day tickets £1 and 50p respectively.

Weekday anglers must obtain day tickets from site office adjacent to car park before proceeding to waters. At weekends only anglers

SWANTON MORLEY LAKE

SWANTON MORLEY fishery in the depths of rural Norfolk has the deserved reputation of being one of the finest roach fisheries in a county blessed with more than a fair share of good roach fishing.

Specimens of more than 2lb are taken regularly from the lakes and from the ¾-mile stretch of the River Wensum which make up the fishery. And for those who like to put together a bag of fish there are plenty in the 8-12oz region to keep them happy for a full day.

Roach are by no means the only fish on offer. Catches often include tench, bream, perch or even a carp or two. And in winter the pike fishing really comes into its own.

River stocks have declined over recent seasons but catches are likely to include specimen dace and chub as well as roach, with always a chance of a wild brown trout to add variety.

Depths in the lakes vary considerably from 3ft to 20ft. Conversely, the smallest lake, nearest the river, has the greatest depth.

The smallest lake at Swanton Morley is also the deepest, with depths up to 20 feet. But it holds an excellent stock of good roach.

Night fishing is not allowed and anglers must be in posession of a valid ticket before commencing to fish, otherwise a £2 penalty is payable.

From Norwich the fishery can be reached via the A1067 Fakenham Road to Bawdeswell; then B1147 to Swanton Morley. Continue past Papermakers public house on left, turning left at next T-junction then sharp right. Go past Waterfall Farm on left and the lakes are 400 yards on the right.

The site is still being worked for sand and gravel and anglers do not have access to the working site or permission to fish in the working lake.

may commence fishing after 8am without tickets and a bailiff will come round.

Ticket details from Ian May, 8 Davis Close, Little Paxton, Hunts, tel: Huntingdon 212059.

OLD BURY HILL LAKE, Dorking, Surrey.
Twelve-acre lake stocked with tench, carp, bream, roach, rudd, pike and zander.

Day tickets only; no season tickets. From June to October tickets cost £2 adults, £1 juniors, OAPs and evenings after 5pm. From November to March, £1 adults, 50p juniors, OAPs and afternoons after 2pm.

Boats available, £2 person extra, and should be booked in advance.

Tickets and boat reservations to Graham Rowles, Lakeview, Old Bury Hill, Westcott, nr Dorking, Surrey, tel: Dorking 883621.

SAVAY LAKE, Moorhall Road, Harefield, nr Denham, Bucks.
Forty-acre lake stocked with specimen carp, tench, perch, bream, pike, roach and rudd.

Day tickets £2 adults, £1 juniors, OAPs and evenings, must be obtained before going onto fishery from Peverills Newsagents, 3 Moorhall Rd, Harefield or Balfours Newsagents, 12 Station Parade, Denham.

Season tickets £20 adults, £10 for juniors and OAPs available from Peter Broxup, 309, Shirland Road, London W9, tel: (01-) 969 6980, by written application only, enclosing sae.

SHERMANBURY PLACE FISHERY, nr Henfield, Sussex.
Two-acre lake containing tench, carp, roach, and rudd, with some trout, ½-mile of River Adur holding bream, chub, roach and trout.

Season tickets £20 adults, £10 juniors and OAPs. Day tickets for limited period of £2 and £1, respectively, to allow anglers to try the fishery.

Enquiries and season ticket requests to Graham Rowles, Lakeview, Old Bury Hill, Dorking Surrey.

SWANTON MORLEY FISHERY, Swanton Morley, nr East Dereham, Norfolk.

Three lakes comprising 65 acres, plus ¾-mile of River Wensum. Roach, carp, eels, pike, perch, pike, rudd and tench in lakes. Roach, dace, chub and trout in river.

Day tickets £1 adults, 50p juniors and OAPs. Season tickets £8 and £4.

Advance day tickets from Chambers, Market Place, Dereham or Rod and Gun, Norwich Street, Dereham, or Mrs V Marsham, Waterfall Farm, Swanton Morley. After 8am tickets should be obtained from Waterfall Farm.

JOIN BOTH AND SAVE CASH!

LEISURE Sport Angling and OWR/Redlands operate a reciprocal arrangement which allows members who wish to join both organisations a healthy discount on season permits.

LSA members qualify for 50 per cent discount, on production of membership card, for all Redlands fisheries. Redlands members get a similar discount for LSA Special Venues which have not reached their rod limits and for all Group Single Water permits. A 25 per cent discount is also offered on LSA group permits covering their 21 group venues.

Discount offers by both organisations do NOT apply to day tickets.

LSA members should enquire about prices and method of application direct to Graham Rowles, Lakeview, Old Bury Hill, Dorking, Surrey.

Redlands members should contact LSA at Thorpe Park, Staines Road, Chertsey, Surrey.

Both organisations reserve the right to withdraw from the offer any single venue that comes under undue angling pressure during the course of a season.

SUCCESS STORY

THE SHARK season had got off to a really poor start. We had fished from the end of May through all of June without a take and we were beginning to think that we might well be in for a repeat of last year when only five shark were boated.

But our skipper, Danny Vokins, is made of stern stuff, and with relentless dedication he drifts the shark grounds off the Isle of Wight in search of the "Big One".

We assembled on Bembridge Angling Club quay at 4.30 am to find what would normally have been a peaceful scene disrupted as 70 anglers prepared to take part in the club's annual Open Shark competition.

By 5.15 we were halfway to the Ledge buoy with the sun just beginning to show above the horizon and the sea rippling gently to a light north-westerly wind. The conditions were perfect.

By 6.45 we were on our mark and spent 30 minutes trying to catch enough fresh mackerel to bait our hooks.

Eventually, the task was completed and we settled down to fish. We took it in turns to lay our rubby dubby trail, using frozen mackerel passed through a mincer mounted on the stern of the boat. It didn't take long to produce a nice oily slick that stretched out behind our drift.

BOB PAKES (left) and skipper Danny Vokins with the new Isle of Wight record thresher shark of 223lb.

RECORD THRESHER ON BROKEN ROD

by BOB PAKES

It was 10.30 before the action started. The shout went up "Shark" and cups of tea were knocked over and discarded sandwiches fell to the deck as we all raced to the gunwale to catch sight of our first shark of the season. It was a porbeagle of about 80lb cruising on the surface nudging the balloon "floats". It passed close to my balloon but my hopes were dashed as the dorsal fin parted my 80lb Dacron like cotton.

No one talked and you could almost hear the other lads praying for it to be on their hook. In the end, Danny's Penn International reel gave us the answer as 70 yards of line was ripped off in one run. Twenty minutes later the first shark slid on to the deck, lightly hooked in the mouth and within three minutes the hook was out and the fish back in the water.

We hunt shark for sport and can see little point in killing such magnificent fish unnecessarily but in general, we keep fish over 100lb as these qualify for the various trophies of the Shark Angling Club of Great Britain.

The next fish also went to Danny and we were beginning to think that we must be doing something wrong when the action stopped dead and for the next 2½ hours nothing happened.

If we were going to reach port for the weigh-in we would have to leave quite soon, but with no fish to take to the scales we decided to stay out but change our position for a new drift seven miles off Ventnor.

Our new drift looked good and within 15 minutes I had my first porbeagle of around 70lb. Two more were caught in the next hour, one at 76 lb the other at 78lb. Both were kept as they earned Jim Primmer and Joaquim Filipe qualification for the SACGB.

I changed my presentation and was now fishing directly below the boat and as I sat contemplating my previous take, the ratchet on my Penn 6/0 clicked twice. Then it clicked twice more. My first thought was that a tope was playing with the bait.

The the fish below started to take line, slowly at first as it went deep, but suddenly the line went slack. My mind was racing — had it let go of the bait or had it started to come up? Before I could make up my mind the water was shattered as a thresher shark leapt 5ft from the water and crashed back sending foam high into the air.

I was in trouble. The fish was on the wrong side of the boat and if the line were to touch the keel I could wave goodbye to my first thresher. The action on the boat became frantic as everybody tried to clear their lines from the water and give me a free hand with the fish.

I dashed to the stern ducking under rods, still not sure if the fish was on. Then my prayers were answered as with a shoulder-wrenching jerk, the line started to fly from the reel. The fish ran astern with terrific speed, stripping 300 yards of line in under a minute. The problem now was to avoid an overrun and I burned my thumb badly trying to check the speed of the free-running spool.

Thankfully, the fish settled and a quick decision had to be made. The fish could just be holding the bait in its mouth but on the other hand with only 50 yards of line left on the spool if it ran again, I would lose it for sure. The decision made, I struck and thankfully felt the hook set hard. For the first time, I could feel the full weight of the fish and I knew it was big.

The fight proper began and for the next half-an-hour line was given and taken on a regular basis. The fish bucked, dived and ran at the boat. My shoulders and forearms were burning and I began to wonder how longer it could go on.

At this point, the last thing you need is a major disaster and you can imagine my horror when mine occurred. I had the shark within 50 yards of the boat, when it ran again and went with such force it fractured my ABU Pacific 8 rod at the lower lock ring.

It took a little while for the full impact of just what had happened to sink in. All I could do was hang on until the run stopped.

When a fish sleeps

by David Gunston

HUMAN and animal sleep is a subject that has received a lot of scientific attention of late but it still has not yielded up all its puzzles and mysteries by any means.

It is difficult for us to believe that any creature of intelligence, living an active life for years, can do without regular sleep but for centuries it was believed that fish did not fall asleep in the way the rest of the animal kingdom does.

The trouble was, and still is, that fish have no opaque eyelids with which to cover their eyes and so they appear always to be awake. There is a theory that most fish lack the mammalian, or reptilian, type of eyelid because the automatic adaptive colour changes in their bodies which blend them to their background are controlled by stimuli received through the eyes. If fish closed their eyes during sleep they would be cut off from this useful protective mechanism.

Of course almost all fish do sleep, though when faced with the blank, open-eyed stare of a fish in a tank, we may find it hard to accept that the creature is more or less unconscious, with nerves and muscles relaxed and as fast asleep as we are at night.

Obviously, a fish's idea of a good sleep may not always correspond too closely with our own, either in duration or deepness, and there are clearly many variations in fish sleep between species and also in different environments, time of the day or year, temperature of the water, and the amount of daylight involved.

Scientists are coming increasingly to the view that sleep is an active rather than the passive function it was for long thought to be: a "switching-on" rather than a "switching off".

The physiology of sleep produces many changes in the living body. Blood pressure and pulse rate decline, respiration becomes slower without losing its basic regularity, there is marked muscular relaxation and almost always a disappearance of powerful reflex actions in response to such stimuli as noise, vibration, light and smell.

All these have been observed in sleeping fish but it is always difficult for us, as creatures conditioned to a lifelong regular 7 to 8 hours of oblivion every night, to imagine any other form of effective sleep — animal sleep, in fact.

Man has actually all but lost some of his original animal abilities in relation to sleep — the ability to "cat-nap", to make do on intermittently broken spells of sleep, many of them of half an hour or less, to combine healthful sleep with some degree of bodily locomotion and activity.

Fish have not lost those abilities and so, to us, their sleep often seems strange, even non-existent. The classic case of a grey nurse shark kept in an Australian aquarium is used from time to time to disprove the view that fish need to sleep at all.

The shark was said to have swum about constantly for six years, swimming some 200,000 ceaseless miles without sleeping — or so it was claimed.

Similarly, if not so spectacularly, long watches were also kept on small captive whales in American marine aquariums with similar results.

In each case, the possibility of a fear-induced restlessness in the creatures, caused by their restriction in captivity, cannot be overlooked but the moving fish must have been otherwise asleep at times, in spite of appearances to the contrary.

Hunger is undoubtedly a factor that can keep a fish awake more effectively than any other. Sight-hunting fish tend to sleep at night and nocturnal feeders during the day. But both will seek food during their normal sleeping periods if they are hungry enough.

It has been known for sleeping grey mullet to be woken by powerful artificial light and to re-form into scavenging shoals and swim on as if daylight had come.

Almost all river fish sleep on or near the bottom and most sea fish prefer to sink lower than their customary level when resting. Flatfish sleep regularly and frequently on their sides on the bottom, often half buried in mud or sand. Lampreys attach themselves by their suckers to a stone or rock when seeking sleep in a swift current.

But many fish undoubtedly sleep, apparently suspended in mid-water without any conscious seeking of resting quarters, although a few oceanic fish, including several sharks and the moon-fish, or opah, sleep on the surface.

Sharks will roll round sideways to sleep and bask in the sun, sometimes ending up with their bellies out of the water. Their spells of sleep may be quite short, lasting minutes rather than hours, and since the shark tribe are notorious for their ability to do without much sleep, those snoozes are sufficient to sustain them for many hours, even days.

Unorthodox positions for sleep are also not unknown. The German scientists Möbius and Heincke kept a wrasse in a tank and noticed that it went to sleep regularly each night lying on its side.

Trigger fish prefer to sleep head downwards and seem to be unique in preferring this position.

The "slippery dick", or Bermuda wrasse, literally goes to bed on the sand bottom and pulls the covers over its head by diving into the soft bottom, giving two or three strong tail wiggles and so concealing itself from view.

Only a small depression in a mound of settled sand reveals where the fish lies, since this gently rises and falls as the gill-openings move during breathing. According to California bioligist Brian Curtis this fish will act in this way even if put in a tank and placed in a darkened room during daylight.

Certain species of fish possess what can best be described as "restful dispositions", in contrast to the restless natures of others.

I then unscrewed the fractured butt and removed it, and unclamped the reel and moved it up the rod blank to within six inches of the bottom roller. With it reclamped in this position I was able to fish on, but had the circumstances been different I would never had got away with it. The last run had drained the last vestiges of strength from the fish which lay deep in the water and waited for my next move.

Taking in line became very difficult as the reel started to twist and I had to steady the rod by pushing my forearm against the bottom roller. The shark bucked several times but never ran again and yard by yard came nearer the boat until after an hour-and-a-half it lay astern.

I took a further 15 minutes to boat the thresher and when it finally hit the deck a great cheer went up from the other lads on the boat. I felt drained and for a while all I could do was sit and look at the fish.

The capture marked the end of the day's fishing and on our return we speculated over the thresher's weight but it was a further 90 minutes before our club scales confirmed a new Isle of Wight record with a fish of 223lb beating the long-standing record of 15 years by 22lb.

LOG

Date: July 7, 1985
Venue: Ventnor, Isle of Wight
Catch: 223lb thresher shark
Captor: Bob Pakes of Ryde

YOU won't find a keener sea angler than ANDREW RACKHAM, who lives near Norwich and is a familiar figure on the beaches of East Anglia when he's not out in a boat! His beach-fishing articles in Angler's Mail weekly drew a big following and we have selected and adapted for the Annual three major features, plus a "special" on Andrew's five basic knots for sea anglers.

ALONG the East Anglian coast, the cod arrive in early October. The first fish are often small or very large and in poor condition but as the month progresses the cod become established and with the rich feeding, soon become prime fish.

The season hits peak at the end of November and carries through to early January, when the larger cod leave the coastline and six weeks later the Spring fish arrive in large quantities.

Among the late Spring cod in April-May are some larger doubles that have spawned and are looking for early peeler crab in the rough ground.

The cod is a storm-beach visitor although they can be found in calm

Preparing for

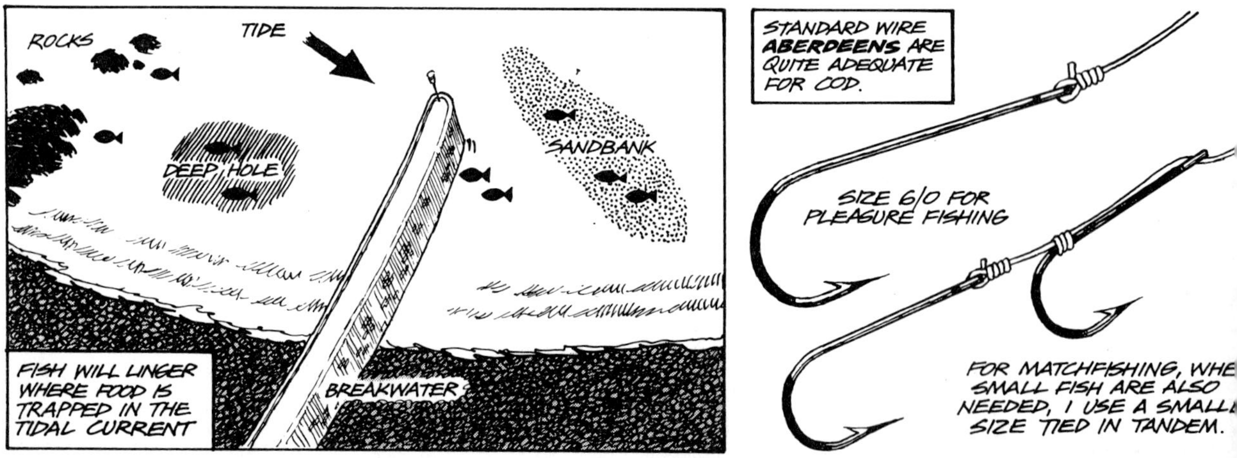

with ANDREW RACKHAM and ARTIST TONY WHIELDON

weather in rocks or strong-tide beaches. During a storm or immediately afterwards is the classic time for the best fishing. During rough weather the murky seas mean that daylight fishing is nearly as good as night-time although the fish do tend to be closer in at night.

Cod fishing is very dependent upon tides. Not only is the right tide on a particular beach important but the fishing definitely improves with stronger tides every fortnight. The prime cod fishing occurs when flood tide is just after dark and the rough weather coincides with a big tide.

Under these conditions be prepared for a bumper catch. Unfortunately however, these conditions rarely coincide and usually it is the use of local knowledge that will guide you to the best fishing conditions.

The cod will run along most beaches and although they can be caught at any distance out they tend to follow the gullies in the sand that hold the food. These gullies can be only 40 or 50 yards from the tideline but along our coastline they are often 130-140 yards out on the best beaches. In rough seas and head winds this gully can be quite a long cast away and this is probably why the pendulum method is so successful in East Anglia.

For better than average catches look for parts of the beach where the fish will linger for some reason or where they will concentrate. Fish will linger where food is trapped in the tide and this can be against breakwaters, in deep holes, against patches of rocks or over sandbanks. The fish will concentrate where the gullies become narrow or where two or more gullies join together.

Cod will eat anything edible and a lot of things that are not, but under most conditions the pleasure angler needs only one bait and that is lugworm. The match angler only needs white rag and the other specialist baits under difficult conditions or at special times of the year.

Big cod have large mouths so a big bait can easily be accommodated. Large baits put out more scent in the tide and attract fish from further afield. They also last longer in the water when crabs are a nuisance.

With the large baits I use large hooks to ensure positive hooking. A size 6/0 will hold a large bait and still look small to cod of 5 lb and above. It also avoids small fish such as dabs and whiting, but if by chance a whiting is hooked, the size of the hook usually means that the fish is lip-hooked and makes excellent live-bait for big cod.

When pleasure fishing I rarely fish with hooks smaller than 6/0 but for matchfishing conditions, when small fish are also needed, a smaller hook is more appropriate. In these circumstances I use two smaller hooks in the same bait, which helps to hook larger fish and still hooks small fish easily.

Basic cod fishing tackle is a simple paternoster rig. The simple rigs are often the best as they are less likely to tangle. A bottom swivel with weight attached and the 18 in. hook snood 2 ft. away from the weight is all that is needed. A bait clip to attach the bait for casting is a refinement that allows the bait to be cast to the gullies in the rough weather.

the cod run

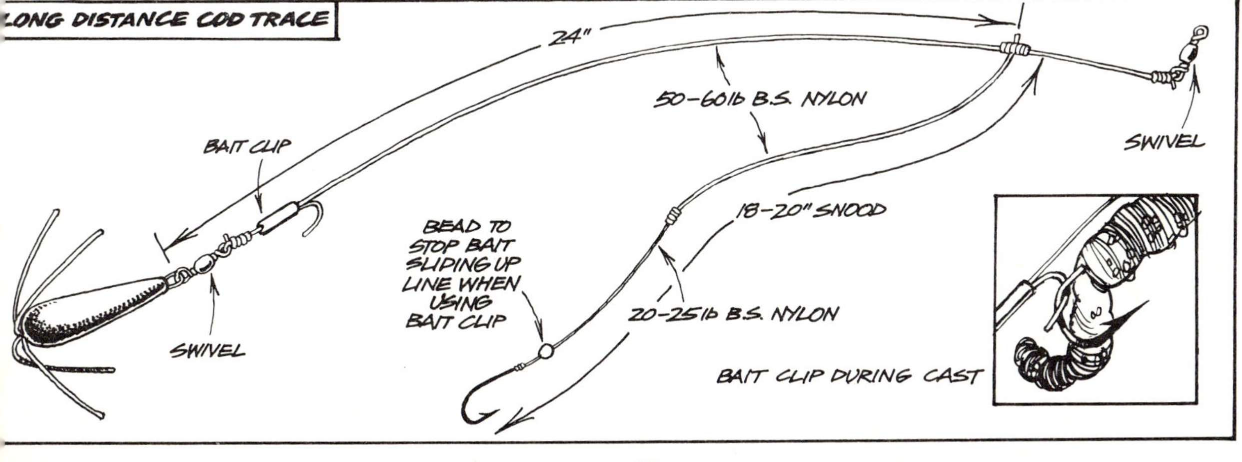

Peelers ha

SUMMER means three important things to the keen shore angler — warm water, peeler crabs shedding their shells and bass moving inshore to feed on the rich harvest.

Bass are found feeding around rocks and sea defences that offer shelter to the crabs which are still soft after losing their hard protective shells. The food source is so rich in protein and so easily traced by the fish that it appears to be the miracle bait when fished under these conditions. For a few heady weeks the bass become so preoccupied with it that they don't seem to have a taste for anything else.

SEARCHING

At low water the crabs shed their shells in the warm-water pools left behind by the tide. The soft new shell is then exposed and as the tide rises the bass will swim up the gullies in search of unprotected crabs that have not managed to find natural shelter.

Bass will swim in surprisingly shallow water during these feeding sorties and sometimes the angler will see bass hunting in water hardly deep enough to cover their dorsal fins. The flood tide or low water period seems to be the most productive time to fish, although bass can turn up at almost any time.

Normal rock-fishing tackle incorporating a nylon paternoster and rotten bottom is all that's needed for most venues. The light link between lead and trace will mean that care has to be taken during casting, but if the weight does become snagged in rocks it can be broken free and the catch reeled in.

MOUNTING

In clear water conditions better results can sometimes be achieved if the peelers are not completely peeled. The top shell is lifted off and the hook nicked through the underside and out of the top. This mounting method looks more natural and has the added bonus of tending to be *less* attractive to smaller fish and especially eels, which can be a problem during the summer.

When the peeler crab explosion subsides the bass move away from the rocks in search of other foods. In storm conditions they can be found foraging in gullies and over sandbanks in search of worms and other food dislodged by the rough sea.

In squally sea conditions, bass follow very similar feeding patterns to cod and can be caught on the same tackle set-up. On surf beaches they move into the surf tables and can be found at extremely close range. The steady breaking surf made up of between five or six waves in succession, produces the surf table and this is where the food gathers between the waves.

If you can pinpoint these pockets of food, then the fish will not be far away. The beach anglers' third wave rule which says that this is the area of most fish activity is often correct.

HUNTING

When bass are not foraging in the surf they will often be found hunting small fish in calmer water. Along with the mackerel, they will follow and feed on whitebait shoals, which are easily lcoated because they attract hundreds of sea-birds hovering over the surface.

Bass will chase their prey to the top and trap them against the surface and I have seen instances where bass have

ve bass appeal

herded thousands of whitebait up against a groyne before attacking them.

Often bass are caught when they are feeding on whitebait by simulating their prey with a spinner. A bright and shiny lure fished deep under the shoals usually has the desired effect.

Bass also hunt sandeels which lie along the edges of sandbanks. A spun sandeel or legered bait is the answer on this type of venue. Excellent sport can be had on spun eels worked across harbour mouths or over sandbanks around estuary mouths.

Harbour bass take on the role of scavenger. They can be caught where scraps of food find their way into the water, and spots around boats or where fish are gutted and sorted are worth a try.

Try to match a harbour bait as closely as possible with the natural food and always present it on lightweight tackle. A bait pinned hard on the harbour bed could look suspicious.

Bass takes are confident but be prepared for bait-robbers like eels and crabs giving a string of rattling bites.

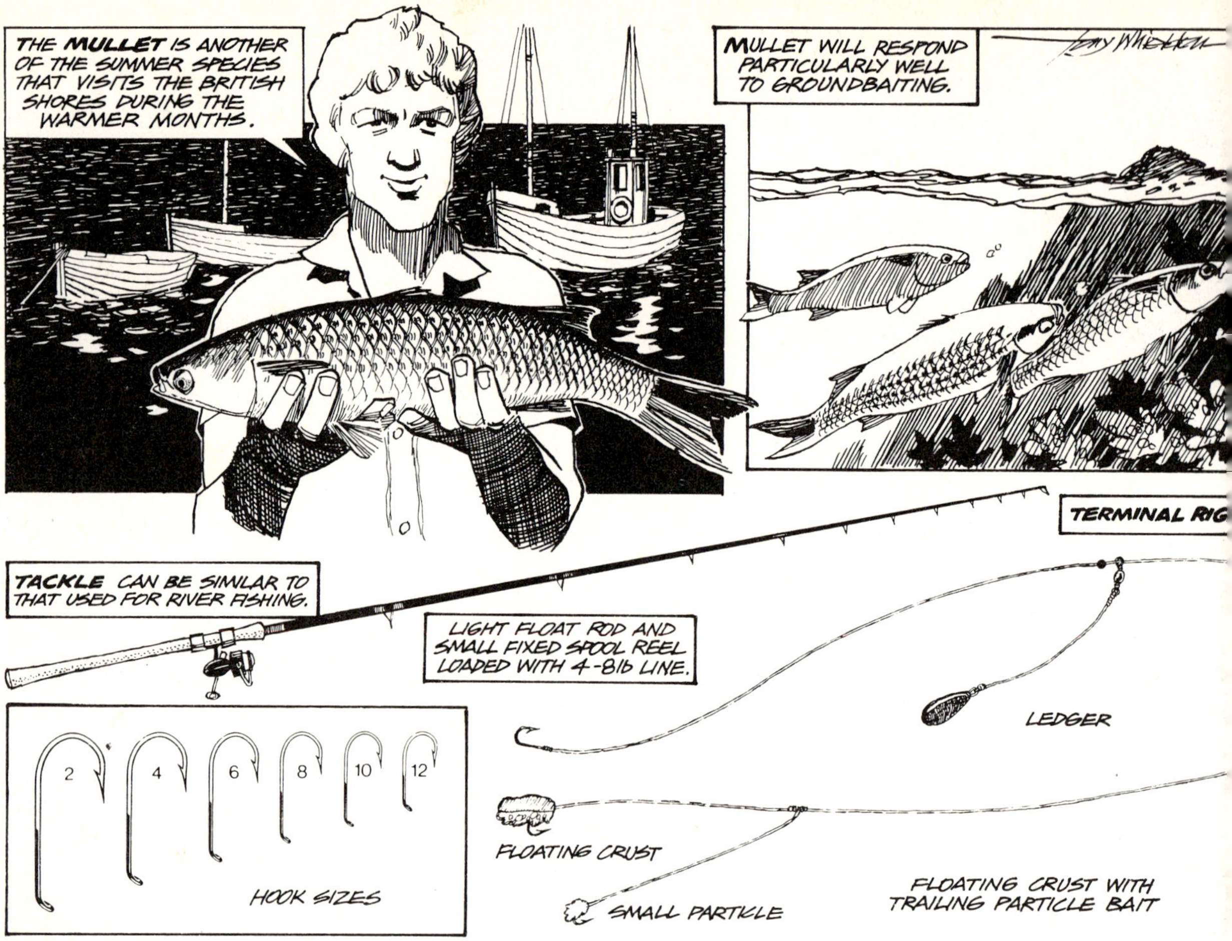

Tempting

MULLET visit British shores during the warmer months and are found around most parts of the coast. They can be caught in the open sea but anglers usually fish for them in brackish estuary waters or around harbour walls.

Mullet tend to be very shy in the "wild" state but they can be amazingly daring once they become "tame" and accustomed to humans. This does not mean however, that they become easier to catch, in fact they can be even more frustrating.

FINICKY

Perhaps it is the finicky ways of the mullet that cause them to be held in such high esteem by anglers.

In their wild state, mullet will feed on small shrimps and creatures found over mud and stones. Over marshland, mullet can be seen taking in mouthfuls of stones and sifting out the food before blowing the rest away. In the "tame" state they can be caught on fish scraps in dock areas.

They will respond particularly well to groundbaiting and they can become "tuned" on to one bait which may be bread, maggots or harbour rag.

If mashed bread is smeared over rocks and mud at low tide, after several days the fish will become used to it. A tethered onion sack containing mashed bread will have a similar effect. A coffee tin with one or two holes punched in the bottom and filled with maggots can be left hung on a post over the water and the maggots will slowly drop in the sea causing quite an attraction to the mullet.

HIDING

Mullet often hide underneath moored boats, sometimes feeding off the fine silkweed attached to the moorings. These areas make excellent fishing venues if permission can be obtained for groundbaiting.

Tackle for mullet can be similar to that used in river fishing. The final choice will depend on the venue but the light tackle will allow the mullet to show off its fighting ability.

BOTTOM

To present bread as a bait offering, you can use either a leger, or a float rig or freeline it into position. If the mullet are visible, then freelining bread can be the most exciting method as the take can be clearly seen.

They can also be caught on bread by using a floating crust as the weight for casting and attaching a smaller hookbait that will sink below the crust as if a small particle had broken away.

When an area has been groundbaited, the mullet can be caught on the bottom using light leger tackle. Small pieces of bread or mag-

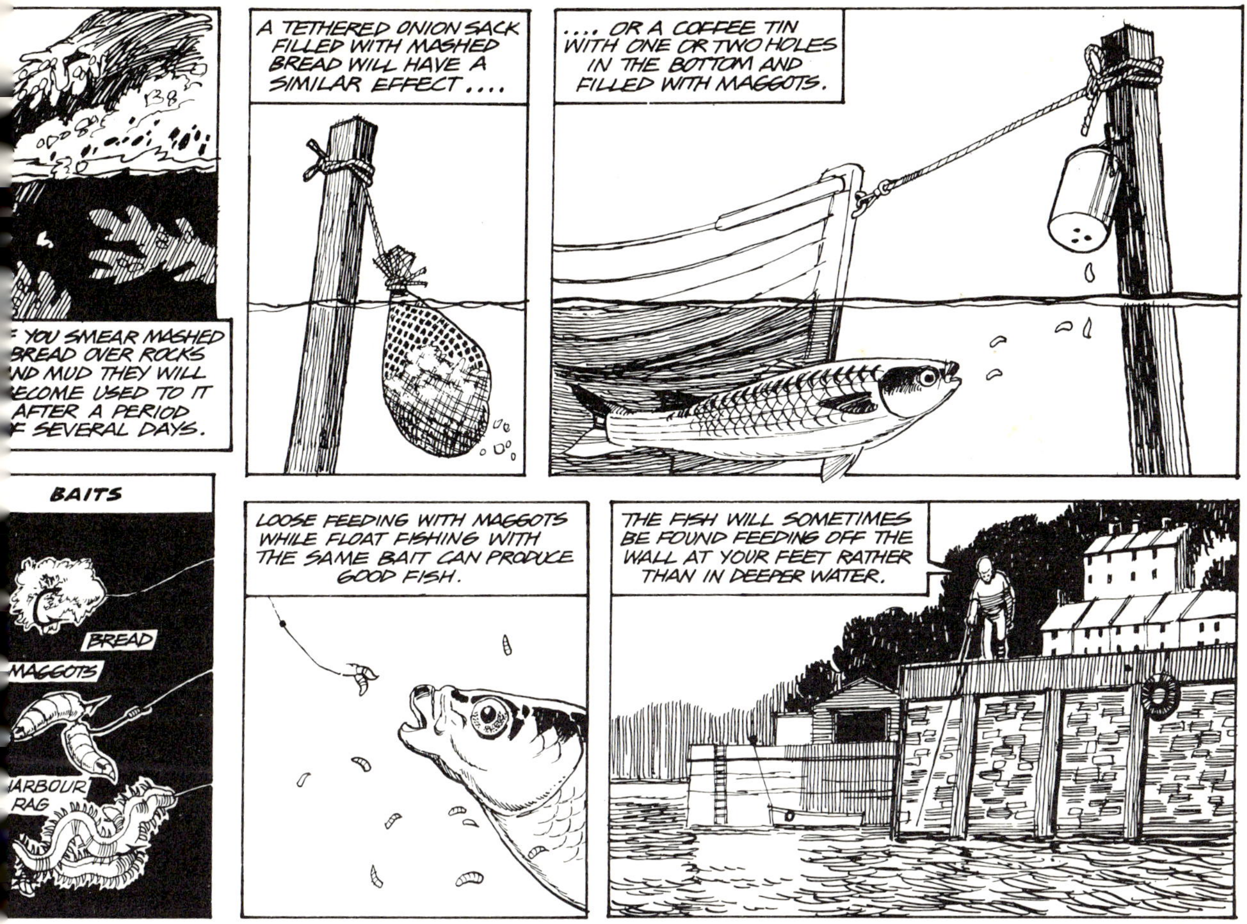

'tame' mullet

gots can be used on the hook depending on the type of groundbaiting that has been carried out. The mullet will also take harbour rag when they are feeding on the bottom.

Float tackle can be used to fish the mid-water marks and loose feeding with maggots while float-fishing with the same bait, can produce good fish which will sometimes be found feeding off the wall at your feet rather than in the deeper water. They will be feeding off the small grubs that inhabit the weed attached to the wall or rocks below. At low water the flies lay their eggs on the rotting weed that is exposed, and the fish are attracted to this as the tide rises.

For most venues the main items of tackle will be a light float rod and small fixed spool reel loaded with line of 4-8 lb depending on the venue. The hook sizes will depend on the bait that is to be presented but they will be in the range of size 12-2.

KNOTS FOR SEA ANGLERS

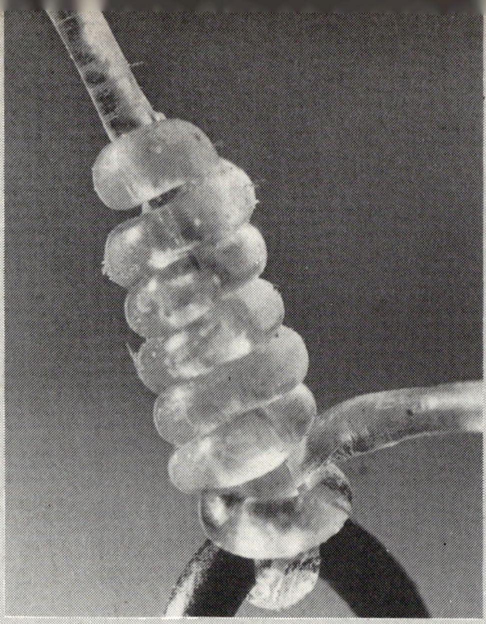

EXPERIENCED anglers often overlook the basic skill of tying knots when they are explaining the techniques of preparing terminal tackle. The secret lies in knowing which knot to use for a specific purpose and how to tie it without damaging the line in the attempt. The second point may sound unimportant but it does require great care to tie a strong knot without damaging the nylon.

The most common cause of knot failure is friction burns caused by pulling a dry nylon knot together. It is always best to wet the line with saliva before pulling tight.

Once the knot has been tied check the nylon for discolouration or mis-shapen diameter which indicates that the knot has been badly tied.

Knots are usually the weakest link in the trace so it is essential that they are tied correctly and checked regularly so that loose leads don't fly off under the full power of a cast.

BLOOD KNOT

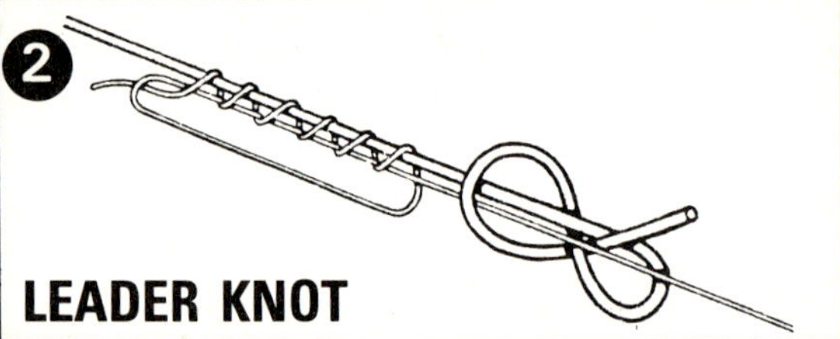

LEADER KNOT

Blood Knot: this is used for joining together lines of approximately the same diameter and is usually employed if the mainline breaks and needs to be rejoined. (Diag. 1).

Leader Knot: the name indicates the use of this knot which is to join the main line to the casting leader which takes the strain of casting. One of the main reasons put forward against using the leader is that weed collects on the joining knot but this drawback is certainly reduced by this small compact knot. (Diag. 2).

Blood Loop: used to form a loop in the trace to which a hook snood can be attached. (Diag. 3).

Half Blood Knot: used to attach swivels or eyed hooks to the snoods. When used with eyed hooks it is useful to give an extra tuck back into the knot. This produces a spur on the eye which holds the bait in place. (Diag. 4).

Double Overhand Knot: used for attaching hook snoods to blood loops. (Diag. 5).

These examples will provide adequate soft knots to cover 90% of all sea angling situations.

ANDREW RACKHAM

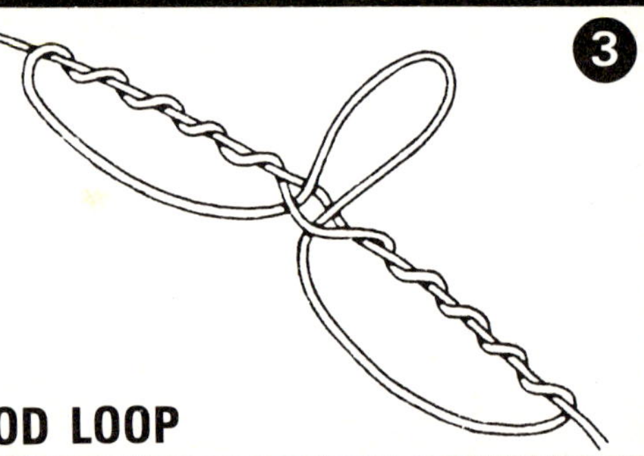

BLOOD LOOP

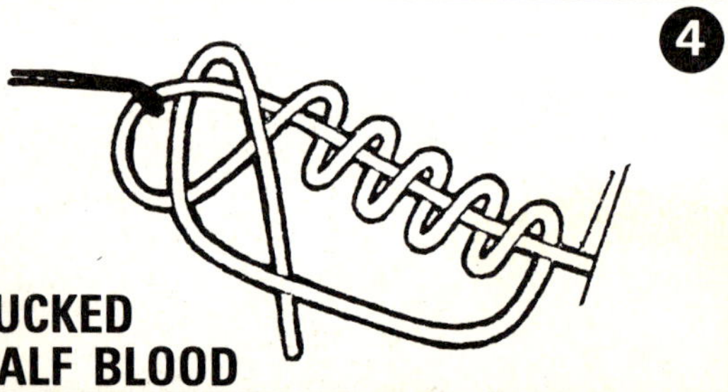

TUCKED HALF BLOOD

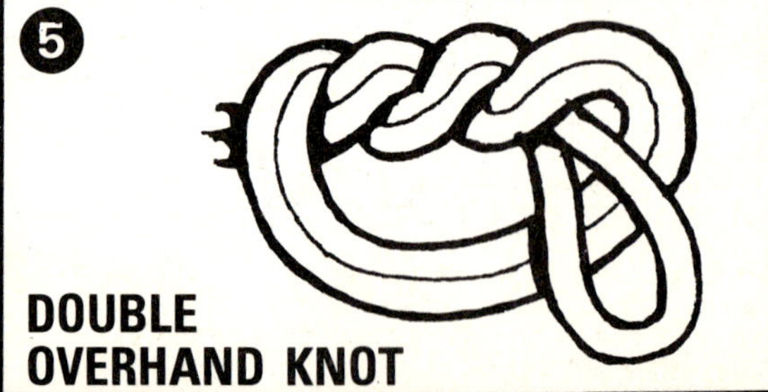

DOUBLE OVERHAND KNOT

I HAVE enjoyed catching coarse fish with a fly rod since my middle teens when I fished the little rivers of Hertfordshire for chub, roach and dace, learning the art of wading slowly and quietly so as not to disturb the fish, of casting accurately first time in impossible situations — and of striking quickly at quick-rising dace and roach.

It was a hard apprenticeship but one which stood me in good stead wherever I have sought both coarse fish and trout on artificial flies.

I love catching grayling on the fly. They are so much harder to hook than any trout, far more cunning, and tremendous fun with standard wet flies or the upstream nymph or shrimp. And yet they are held in far less esteem than the generally more stupid trout.

Chub, too, are super fish to tempt on a fly, particularly dry flies such as Mayflies, Sedges, Palmers or Daddy Long Legs, and especially during that productive last hour before dark.

A few years back I tied up a whole

John Wilson unhooks a 4lb. Norfolk Wensum chub taken on a Mayfly nymph.

FLY FISHING FOR COARSE FISH

BY JOHN WILSON

batch of enormous 2-3 inch long flies from spun deer hair, similar to the Muddler Minnow pattern much-loved by stillwater trout anglers.

When jerked across the surface those monstrosities simulated a shrew or baby vole and though they never attracted many takes, when they came they were usually from a good pike or a large chub.

Pike are caught regularly on basic fly patterns on our big reservoirs where fish of 20lb-plus often fall to light fly outfits intended for browns or rainbows. I have taken pike to over 16lb on a 9ft 2oz carbon fly rod and what a thrilling scrap they provide!

Roach and rudd can be tempted at times with a dry fly or slowly-sinking nymph, particularly on warm summer evenings. Rudd are very free risers and quite large specimens can be taken.

But if it has to be admitted that catching coarse fish on a fly is a good deal harder than by conventional methods it is consequently much more satisfying to me.

Sunken nymphs usually offer the best chance and it was with this in mind that I went down to try my luck on a local stretch of the River Wensum in Norfolk, one afternoon in autumn.

Conditions were far from ideal. The river was flowing crystal clear without a hint of colour, and weed was everywhere, growing almost bank to bank. But, nothing ventured, nothing gained, so I put up my favourite two-piece carbon fly wand, plus a light reel holding a double-taper floating line.

I tied a size 8 Mayfly nymph to the business end of a 5lb leader. First cast between two beds of submerged weeds brought a quick pull and with a turn of the wrist I was soon landing a small dace, the large artificial looking ridiculous in its small mouth.

Several more dace and a small chub followed before a fish hit the nymph with a bang and shot off upstream, taking with it line which I had coiled at my feet on the bank.

The light rod hooped right over and quickly took the sting out of the fish — a chub of over 4lb. A couple of minutes later and it was mine, safely in the landing net at the first attempt.

As I unhooked it with a pair of artery forceps, I mused over the fact that the chub — no stranger to anglers' baits and unlikely to have taken conventional baits until much later in the day — should fall to the unlikely Mayfly nymph. But, then, isn't the unexpected what angling is all about?

This tackle is more commonly seen on a trout lake but it can account effectively for coarse fish, including the chub that is almost ready for a brief trip ashore in a landing net.

HOLIDAY FISHING

TREVOR HOUSBY IN

My fight wi
856lb. MA

TREVOR HOUSBY, of Lymington, Hampshire, visits the Azores Islands every year as angling consultant to the Portuguese Tourist Board and never misses a chance to search for the giant blue and white marlin that roam the islands' mid-Atlantic waters. But Trevor's catches, during his 1985 visit, exceeded even his wildest dreams when he landed eight big marlin in eight days, finishing on the last afternoon with a European record-breaking monster of 856lb. that took 1½ hours to tame. This is Trevor's personal account of his thrilling adventures.

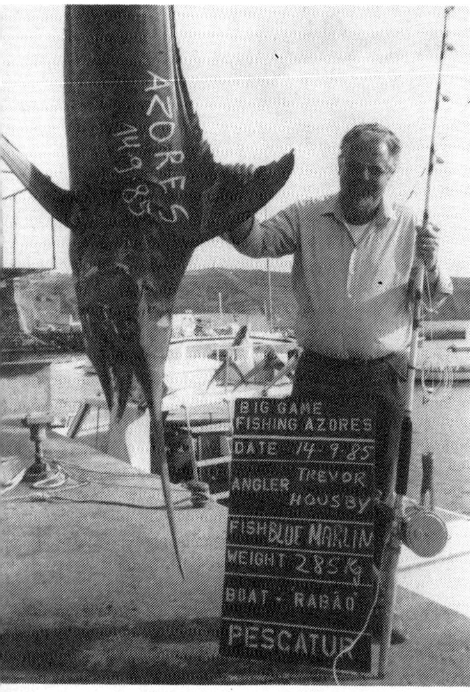

A whopper by any big-game hunter's standards but Trevor's 628lb (285k) marlin was dwarfed by his later catch of the 856lb record-breaker.

Sheffield tackle dealer Terry Smith with his 50lb bream haul.

Bream in Sweden run big — but study the picture and guess the size of the pike that took a bite out of this near-4lb specimen.

Angling journalist Don Bridgewood and Terry Smith show the quality of bream they caught in a stillwater near the Swedish town of Gnosjo.

Bream, roach, skimmers and a few perch came from the "off" and I reckon I had only one cast without getting a bite, which were shy because of cold weather that kept our catches down during our five-day visit.

A long journey south found us at a village called Bledingsholm for one day. Not a lot caught there but enough to prove that on a day when we didn't need thermals it had a lot of potential from the river, canals, dykes and lakes which make up what will be a venue specially for anglers by the time you read this.

Martin had visited the place earlier in the season in June and in the warmer weather caught tench to 4lb, bream of a similar weight and good roach.

Pike and zander, plus a sprinkling of carp, make up the other main coarse fish stocks of a country that has an unbelievable 56,000 lakes to choose from.

I have already mentioned the need for pre-baiting — but also take heed of the locals. They do know where the fish live but their methods are not the same as ours and they do not, generally, take such big catches.

They were very interested in our running-line methods, which are still in their infancy in Sweden. When they get them right there could be some eye-opening catches from anglers who are restricted, most of the time, to pole fishing.

Details of Swedish angling are obtainable from Martin Founds, Anglers World Holidays, 25 Market Place, Bolsover, Chesterfield, Derbyshire.

The fir-lined Nissan lake system in Sweden is full of big bream, say the Angler's Mail visitors.

HOLIDAY FISHING

TREVOR HOUSBY IN

My fight w
856lb. MA

TREVOR HOUSBY, of Lymington, Hampshire, visits the Azores Islands every year as angling consultant to the Portuguese Tourist Board and never misses a chance to search for the giant blue and white marlin that roam the islands' mid-Atlantic waters. But Trevor's catches, during his 1985 visit, exceeded even his wildest dreams when he landed eight big marlin in eight days, finishing on the last afternoon with a European record-breaking monster of 856lb. that took 1½ hours to tame.
This is Trevor's personal account of his thrilling adventures.

A whopper by any big-game hunter's standards but Trevor's 628lb (285k) marlin was dwarfed by his later catch of the 856lb record-breaker.

th an RLIN!

WALKING down to the dock in hot September sunshine I marvelled yet again at the lovely Atlantic islands of the Azores. Beneath my feet the black and white mosaics of Fayal Island; beyond, across six miles of blue water lay Pico with its vast Fujiyama-shaped mountain. And to complete the triangle San Jorge island, with its towering cliffs, lay stark and clear in the clean air.

Climbing aboard the Pescatur big game boat, "Rabao", I was again conscious of the magnificent fishing already behind me. In eight days we had caught three white and three blue marlin, two of which had weighed over 750lb. Now, on my last day of the expedition, I hoped for great things.

Clearing the harbour entrance we ran out three Kona head type lures and began the long haul out to the Bank of the Condor, which, in reality, is the tip of a submerged mountain and a plateau so rich in food fish that it attracts huge predatory fish of many kinds.

In a five-year period the Condor Bank has been kind to me. Over its unseen peak I have caught large shark of many kinds, including several record-breakers. Only the day before I had boated a 660lb. blue marlin and now, with glass-calm conditions, I hoped for a monster.

Nearing the Condor the sea tuned dark indigo. Blue water like this always holds fish and within minutes the first marlin was up, slashing frantically at the fast-moving lure. Seconds later it was hooked up and running, the 9-0 Everoll reel screaming and smoking as the fish ran hard and fast downtide.

I saw the fish clearly as it hammered at the bait and knew it was not a monster, my estimate was somewhere between 250 and 300lb.

With this first fish in the boat I felt fit and relaxed, ready for anything. What I did not count on was two marlin hooked up at the same time! As my fish jumped its way into the middle distance I suddenly saw a big marlin jumping within yards of the boat. Worse, it had a Kona head swinging from the jaw and a great bunch of my line in its mouth. Fortunately, both fish shook free of the lures before a breakage occurred.

Lures raise more fish than "naturals" but they lose more as well. When a marlin sucks in a natural bait the texture and taste mean it will hang on to the bait but the second it closes its jaws on a plastic lure it knows it has made a mistake.

By 4 p.m. we had hooked and jumped off more marlin than most anglers see in a lifetime and with 5 o'clock set as the agreed quitting time it looked as if I would have to be content with the one fish.

For a while nothing happened. Then out of nowhere a huge fish appeared directly astern of a big blue Kona head.

When a blue marlin makes up its mind to attack its whole body lights up like a blue neon sign and this fish came up fast, threw the lights on and hit the bait so hard that I thought the rod would snap.

Instantly, it turned and went smoking off downtide in a display of raw temper that had to be seen to be believed. Lifting the bucking rod from its own socket I jammed the rod tip hard back, hopefully to set the hook solidly. This action angered the fish beyond all reason and it began to jump as it ran.

With friction smoke pouring from the reel I slid gratefully into the fighting chair, put the rod butt into the gimble, snapped my shoulder harness clips on to the reel lugs and settled back for the brutal work ahead.

On its first run, the fish took over 500 metres of line off the reel, jumping more than 50 times in the process, until it realised that jumping would not get rid of the dangling lure. Then it dived deep, allowing me to recover over 300 metres of line in the process and with the boat virtually above the fish I was able to apply maximum rod pressure.

Twenty minutes later it was back on top, tailwalking towards the horizon in a defiant show of strength and temper that I had little opportunity to admire.

When these tactics failed yet again the fish went down deep and started to hand out as much punishment as it could and twice lifted me to a semi-standing position in the fighting chair.

By now it was giving line grudgingly. I would win 20 yards, then lose 15 but each time I filled the reel spool a little more. At the end of the first hour the double line was in sight but not yet inside the rod rings.

The slow lift and rapid wind down routine was, by now, totally automatic. If the fish took line, I forced it to fight for every inch. Then, when it paused, I built up the pressure to bring it back up.

Finally it was over, the leader swivel snicked against the top roller ring and the huge fish rolled up beside the boat. No-one had to tell me that it was a record-breaker. I could see from its length, girth and huge bill that it was a monster.

Three of us pulled full strength but it was impossible to get the fish inside the boat. Instead, we tied it alongside for the long steam back.

In all, I had fought the fish for only 1½ hours, although marlin of this size are normally classed as three or four hour fish. My own strength and years of big fish experience had helped me cut the fighting time in half.

Arriving in Horta at 10 p.m. we had to use a crane to lift the fish into the boat, but now the sadness started, for it was too late for weighing and I had to be at the airport at first light. And as it was a Sunday night I had no way of changing my tickets.

Next morning I hurried to the boat to photograph and then leave my best-ever blue marlin.

My estimate of weight was between 850 and 900lb. Two days later I was contacted by the Portuguese Tourist office who told me the official weight was 856lb — 18 hours after capture!

Since that first call all necessary papers have been forwarded to me and record claims filed. If all goes well my name will stand against this magnificent fish and two other species taken during that same trip — the white marlin record (European) and the Wahoo record (European).

The notice board says it all ... This is the 856lb (388 kilos) European record marlin captured by Trevor Housby on the last afternoon of his visit to the mid-Atlantic Azores islands. But Trevor failed to make next morning's traditional quayside photo-call because he was already high above the Atlantic, flying home to Lymington, Hampshire.

WHAT IT COSTS

A BIG-GAME fishing trip to the Azores varies in overall costs, depending on which tour operator is used. But Trevor Housby's cost guidelines give a fair idea of how deep you need to dig for an 8-day (seven nights) stay, including boat charges.

	£
Charter flight from UK to Azores, via Lisbon	220
Room in a 4-star hotel for 7 nights	140
Meals (very cheap, reports Trevor)	50
Boat charter – 200 US dollars per day, shared between, say, 4 anglers for 7 days, at current exchange rates gives approx cost per head	240
Total estimated cost per person	£650

Costs can be cut significantly if bed and breakfast accommodation is acceptable, instead of a 4-star hotel — and if you shop for cheapest flight available. Some firms now offer complete "packages" for Azores holidays.

Further information from Portuguese National Tourist Office, 1 New Bond Street, London W1. Tel. 01-493 3873.

Where to catch a 68½ pounder!

MAX COTTIS had only one ambition when he boarded the Channel Ferry for the Continent — to beat his personal best carp of 26lb. Little did he realise that four days later, at Lake Cassien in the blazing June heat of Southern France, he would almost triple that target with a 68½lb. monster mirror that made him one of the most talked-about men in angling.

The story starts at Max's home in Newbury Park, Essex, when he saw a picture of a 49½lb. carp landed at Lake Cassien by Don Smith, of Clacton, who was one of the first British anglers to go it alone at the French venue.

"When I saw that picture I thought 'I must have some of that' and started planning the trip from that moment", says Max, who got together with Keith Selleck of Middlesex Angling Centre.

They decided to go to France in the English Close Season as they didn't want to miss out on any fishing at home and set a date for the beginning of June.

He and Keith spent their evenings sorting out all the details of the trip, planning routes and working out costs for petrol, motorway tolls and the ferry.

"We had some help from anglers who had been to Cassien before but, obviously, they weren't going to give away all their own secrets so we worked blind in a lot of areas", Max recalls.

"I think a lot of people have got the wrong idea about the lake — they believe they can go over there and just drag 30-pounders in all day long. But it doesn't happen like that. Lake Cassien is huge, with more than 1,300 acres, and there are miles of unfished banks. So finding the fish in the first place is very difficult".

Because of the vast acreage Max had been advised to fill his swim with bait to stand more of a chance of attracting the big carp to his area and that meant preparing thousands of boilie baits.

He used Micky Richardson's Supa-mix, which he had tried and tested at local Essex venues. This takes about five eggs for a 10oz. mix, so Max got through 180 eggs in preparing 5,000 boilies.

"The food processor was almost in flames by the time I had finished," he jokes.

Max and Keith invited their friends Alan Bradley and Diana Alabaster to join the trip and decided to tow a caravan through France as the cheapest and best means of organising the trip.

But they were decidedly not looking forward to the gruelling and monotonous 27-hour drive to Lake Cassien, which included driving around aimlessly for three hours when they got hopelessly lost. But, at least, Cus-

IF only this was a leafy swim at an English carp lake! The 68½-pounder, which Max Cottis, of Newbury Park, Essex, is struggling to control for the camera, would then rank as an instant national record-breaker. But this picture was taken at Lake Cassien, in the South of France, where Max and his pals enjoyed a remarkable session with heavyweigts.

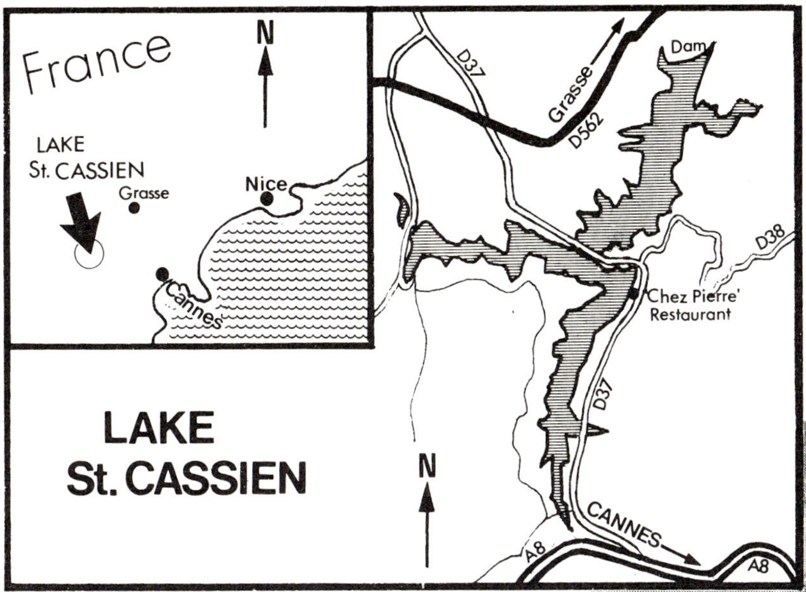

toms officials turned a blind eye to the huge bags of boilies they were carrying!

The group made camp near Chez Pierre's, a cafe on the banks of Lake Cassien where previous parties had stayed, and Max wasted no time in filling his swim with bait.

For three days they waited for a fish but a lift bite for Max provided the only stir. They persevered until the third day and then decided the only thing to do was to try another swim.

"Originally, we planned for the trip to last seven days but, eventually, we had to extend it to ten because the first part of the trip was unproductive," says Max.

On the fourth morning luck changed as Max found the fish — even if he wasn't quite ready "I was lying down when I heard the fish crashing about the baits and then suddenly the monkey climbers shot up".

Cassien carp are not at all finnicky, as Max found out with a screaming first run.

"The fish just charged off and I knew it was a big one — but as I had only caught fish to 26lb before I really had no idea how big it was. Judging by that first run I thought it could go 35 maybe 40lb."

Max was fishing about 10ft. from the bank on a rock plateau, about 7ft deep, and when the mirror picked up the bait it crash-dived into a depth of about 30ft with line grating over the rock bar, demanding extreme care in playing.

Since Max's visit, others have found that the easiest way to deal with Cassien's huge fish is to jump into a boat and follow their long, powerful runs but Max could only stand on the bank and hold on. And having chosen a new swim he was some distance away from the rest of the group and his calls for help went unheard.

The carp fought on for 1¾ hours before it tired enough for Max to get it within sight of the bank and then into his net.

"I was shaking all over and had to sit down and get over the shock before I could even think of looking for the others," admits Max, who still had no precise idea of the weight.

"I found Keith and told him the fish might go 50lb. but when we put it on our 55lb. scales it went down straight to their limit. Then we tried the 112lb. set and I was truly amazed to see the weight settle at 68½lb".

After photographs had been taken the fish was returned gently to the lake — much to the disgust of some French onlookers who believe that carp are for the pot!

A 47lb. 3oz Cassien carp, caught by Max Cottis, goes back with care. French onlookers, who regard big carp as intended for a big pot, are amazed when English anglers return their catches.

Next day Max landed a 17lb. carp and followed that an hour later with another whopper of 47lb. 3oz.

But that still wasn't enough for the man who had taken the heaviest carp ever recorded by a British angler. On his return to Essex he was soon discussing another trip — with thoughts of a 100-pounder!

THE CASSIEN 68½lb. CARP RIG

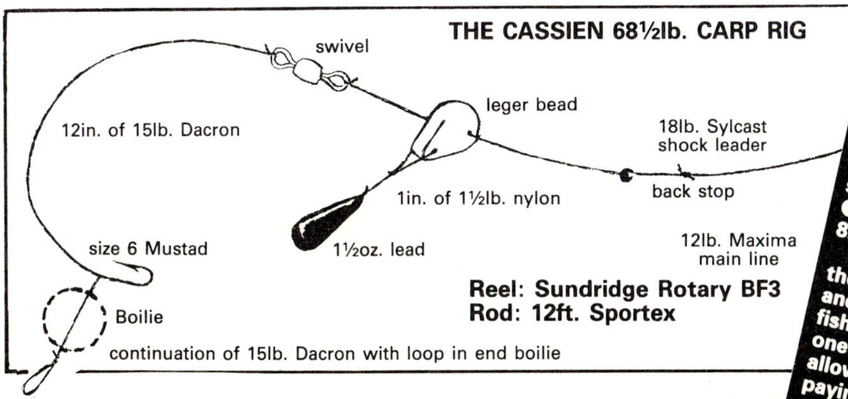

Reel: Sundridge Rotary BF3
Rod: 12ft. Sportex

STICK TO THE RULES — OR ELSE

FRENCH Authorities welcome British angling tourists to Cassien provided the rules are followed to the letter:

- **NO nightfishing.**
- **NO camping on the lakeside. There are camp sites only two miles away.**
- **NO more than one rod from April 15 until after June 15, when up to three are allowed.**
- **NO sleeping in car parks surrounding the lake.**
- **NO anglers on the lake before sunrise.**
- **NO anglers to remain after 8.30pm.**

Failure to follow the rules led to the arrest of two English anglers and confiscation of their tackle for fishing at night with more than one rod. They were released and allowed to continue fishing after paying fines to the police.

LIFE AFTER

MOST of the lead weights used in coarse fishing have got to be eliminated by 1987. If this is not achieved voluntarily the Government is expected to introduce a ban that will be enforced through bye-laws operated by the various Regional Water Authorities which issue rod licences. *Angler's Mail* has campaigned vigorously in 1986 for a voluntary switch to tried and tested acceptable non-toxic alternatives now available in the shops. The *Mail's* special reports on the best of these alternatives are here condensed and adapted as a review with an urgent recommendation to give them a try.

SAFEWEIGHTS

WIMET LTD, had issued nearly six tons of Safeweights to the tackle trade by January 1986 and have the capacity to make many tons more.

The Coventry-based company has invested over £15,000 in developing their product and in tooling-up for production.

The idea for a shot made from tungsten to replace lead came from Wimet managing director Geoff Whitehouse, who realised the two materials had similar properties.

But the man who made the idea work was Andy Hayward, Wimet's chief designer, who devised a copper hinge to fit inside the tungsten shot to give it strength.

Malcolm Hughes, commercial manager, says: "Since the initial design, we have modified and improved the product by adding protrusions inside the split in the shot to prevent it slipping down the line.

This was one of the criticisms of our earlier design which, we are certain, we have now put right."

Wimet have gone down as far as No. 6 shot but have no plans to produce a smaller shot — they say it is just not practical with their design.

Says Mr Hughes: "We tried to get down to a size 8 in laboratory conditions but it just wouldn't work.

"When the Coventry Safeweight National Squad want to use a shot smaller than size 6, they break off a small piece of our malleable tunsten putty to make up weights as small as 10, 11 and 12.

"They find this is not only better than lead when fishing fine, as it doesn't damage the line, but it is much easier than lead to move up and down."

All seven sizes of Safeweight are sold in these plastic dispensers. Also pictured here are the new tungsten bombs which will not be marketed until it is clear just what will be outlawed.

SAFEWEIGHT PRICES

Single size boxes, from SSG down to No. 6 sell for recommended retail price of £1.65. A box of four different sizes is £2.29. A Wimet dispenser containing all seven sizes of their shot was introduced last February at £2.99.

AAA and BB Safeweights (top) shown fixed above lead shot of identical weight. There is no difference in size.

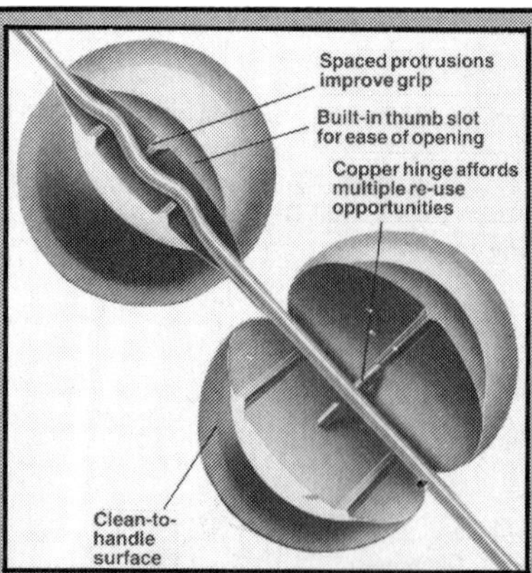

How the hinge action works.

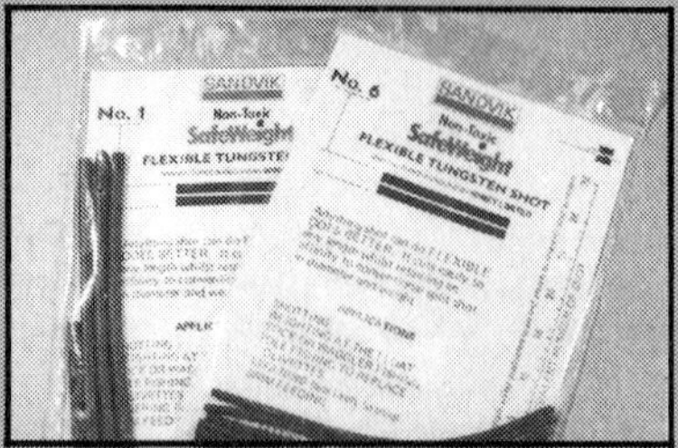

Safeweight's flexible shot is useful for bulk shot or for increasing the weight on a swimfeeder.

LEAD SHOT

THAMESLEY SURE SHOT

Sure Shot in front of its unique spillproof container.

THAMESLY are convinced that they are on a winner with their Sure Shot lead substitute - and the FOUR TONS they have sold since September 1985 suggests they could be right.

Early criticism that Sure Shot was too bright, led to the East London based firm dulling it with non-toxic graphite.

Thamesly are now so confident that their new-look product is as good as, if not better, than lead shot, that they have announced plans to produce it down to a No.4.

"When we first brought it out we made just three sizes — SSG, AAA and BB. But now we will be producing No.1 and No.4s as well and we'll be marketing the new sizes as soon as possible," said managing director Bernie Bristow.

"No.4 seems to be the limit. We don't think we will be able to get down to a No.6 but we see the new sizes as a major breakthrough," he said.

Sure Shot comes in the spill-proof, single-shot dispensers that Thamesly developed for their conventional lead shot and at present Sure Shot retails at £1.60 per container.

Thamesly spent 12 months developing their product having been pressurised into producing a lead alternative because 95 per cent of their business revolved around the lead shot market.

"We had to come up with an alternative — lead shot was our livelihood," said Bernie Bristow.

Their efforts produced a material that looked and felt like a harder version of lead and which has similar properties.

Sure Shot is easy to pinch on the line, with no tweezers or biting required, and it can be removed with the thumbnail. One tackle shop in East London invited customers to try opening one of the new Sure Shot — and they did it, 1,500 times!

Said Bernie Bristow: "We have proved our product is 50 times more durable than lead and can be re-used many times, so anglers should not have to keep buying supplies as they did with lead shot.

"I have had letters from the tackle trade congratulating us on our shot, so someone obviously thinks we have got it right.

TOP OF THE MARKET

STUART ARNOLD, skipper of Division One National champions ABC, has won two matches this season using Sure Shot and rates it highly.

"If they banned lead tomorrow I would use Sure Shot before anything else on the market," he said. "I use it as locking shot with wagglers and have found it very good."

"It's pure tin, which is why it is so like lead and also so expensive, but it is certainly a good substitute and slides easily up and down the line without weakening it," said Stuart.

He was not sure, however, that the complete answer in terms of a lead substitute had yet been found.

"No.6 is the most crucial size in match fishing and there isn't a good alternative on the market in that size. Until there is, I don't think the problem has been solved."

The three size of Sure Shot with their lead equivalents. As can be seen, the substitutes are slightly larger.

POSITIVE REACTION

NFA boss Joe Betteridge reveals that a test panel employed by the Federation were more impressed with Thamesly Sure Shot than any other substitute.

"We had a very positive reaction from our panel who used it in all types of fishing and came up with encouraging results.

"I use Sure Shot in my own fishing and find that despite arthritic fingers I can squeeze it easily on the line, something I was never able to do with lead," said Joe.

EASY TO FIX

SAFEWEIGHTS will grip the line by finger pressure alone but if you don't have "hard" fingers, through working in an office, for instance, a small pair of tweezers will do the job. You can even bite on the weights — but do it gently. Do it too hard and you will end up with a mouthful of dust.

● DON'T open up the gap in the shot any further or you will destroy the hinge action.

● TAKE care when re-opening that the gap is just sufficient to free the line. Handled carefully in this way, Safeweights can be re-positioned or re-used very easily.

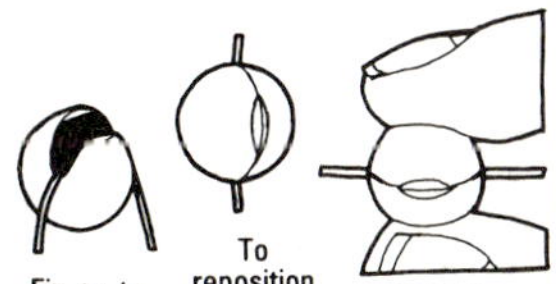

Fix on to slack line, with line held against hinge. | To reposition on line, do not slide. Open carefully — move — close. | Only use fingers or plastic pliers to close.

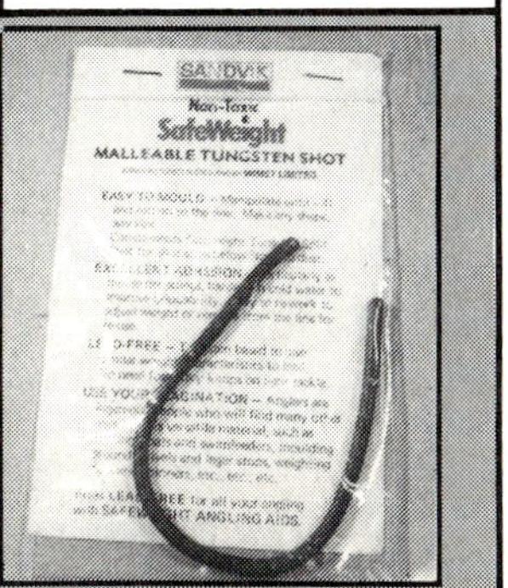

Safeweight's malleable shot can be used for sizes as small as No. 10 or 11.

OTHER OPTIONS

THERE are various other alternatives to lead shot on the market which anglers should try in a personal search for the substitute that will enable them to carry on fishing.

These include — EVODE ANGLERS' WEIGHT, a mixture of stainless steel compound in a malleable rubber base. In use, a piece of the compound can be rolled into a desired size or shape.

LAMMIMAN COILED SHOT is available in sizes from Swan down to No.10 and relies on the line being wound on to it at both ends.

SATURN SHOT is a zinc-related steel product available in larger sizes (SSG, AA, BB) with smaller sizes (No.3s and 6s) for use as dropper shot.

The din of 15,000 chickens at Dorrington, Lincolnshire, has been replaced by a deafening silence! Here's the first lake, which contains 7,000 bream.

THE LOCO THAT STOPS AT EVERY PEG...

Tackle deliveries by train ... direct to your peg. All part of the service at the new Dorrington coarse fishery run by Mavis Hall.

FISH have given 15,000 fowl the elbow down on the farm at Dorrington in Lincolnshire. The chickens got the chop once Tim Hall and his mother, Mavis, decided to flatten their poultry farm and excavate day-ticket coarse fishing lakes in their place.

The first pond has been stocked with a mixed head of fish including 7,000 bream to 4lb, tench and chub. Now Tim is developing a second water in which he hopes to release a fast growing strain of carp.

But at least one feature of the poultry farm will remain on site — an impressive 3½ ton Ruston and Hornsby locomotive. A railway track runs right around the fishery and the loco will be used to send anglers' tackle right to their peg.

The engine is the only one of its type left in the British Isles still working as an agricultural locomotive. The diesel was built in Lincoln in 1954.

Water for the fisheries is being supplied by a windmill on the farm which has been built by Tim Hall. "The windmill will pump approximately 42,000 gallons of water a week from a nearby stream which is fed by three artesian wells which have never been known to dry up" says Tim.

When the carp lake has been dug, Tim has advised his mother to have another small pond stocked with Koi carp to sell as ornamental fish.

If the coarse fishing project is a success Mavis Hall may well open up yet another fishery in an adjoining field.

Shower facilities and toilets are already available to anglers. Two permanent caravans can be hired and eventually, standings will be made alongside the car park for anglers to take their own caravans.

"We don't know at this stage whether to let the coarse lakes to a club or keep them on a day-ticket basis as they are now. It will depend on how popular the waters become," added Tim.

Day-tickets from 7am to 7pm cost £2, 4pm to dark £1. Telephone bookings can be taken at (0526) 832327.

RODNEY COLDRON

NIGHT fishing from a beach has a special attraction that stirs the imagination of even the most experienced angler. But when you are only 15 years old the excitement can be intense as dusk deepens...what hidden "monster" is lurking only a short cast from the shore, waiting to pounce on your bait?

This youngster, who is fishing a late evening tide at Dengemarsh, in Kent, knows that at any second his rod top could pull over hard to signal a bite and makes sure he is ready for the call by grasping the butt firmly.

PICTURE: DAVID SELLMAN

The dawn of a new coarse fishing season is like no other date in the angling calendar. More planning and preparation will go into that first trip than any other. And hopes will be higher than on all the other outings to come.

That is why June 16 has a special place in the hearts of all who enjoy coarse fishing and it will probably remain so, whatever changes to the Close Season the future may hold.

But once all the hard work is out of the way, a favourite swim baited up and the first cast made, there's nothing left to do but to settle down to the waiting game. That, at least, will never change!

PICTURE: KEVIN SMITH

ALL AT SEA!

Deepsea wreck-fishing is a tough sport. Concentration, physical strength and reserves of stamina, plus a strong stomach and good sea legs are all essentials. But the rewards can be great when a shoal of big cod or pollack are located.

This angler is putting his back into steering a large cod away from the superstructure of a wreck lying many fathoms below. His task now is to winch the fish to the surface as quickly as possible so that no time is wasted in dropping a fresh bait down to the wreck for another tiring battle... and then another...

● *Turn to page 41 for Mike Millman's advice on techniques needed to tackle big fish from a boat.*

PICTURES: MIKE MILLMAN

A 23½lb. cod comes aboard on 20lb. test tackle. Light-line fishing increases sport with big fish but should never be so light that fish are needlessly lost.

Carp anglers are a breed apart — highly dedicated, often secretive and withdrawn individuals with talk that usually centres around tales of "twenties" and "thirties" or the latest boilie mix.

Len Head, from Great Cornard, Suffolk, admits that he prefers the solitude of night-fishing and for days at a time, work permitting. But when he records a catch like this, the hours and effort are repaid.

He went to a favourite Essex gravel pit, at the height of the summer, to land this mixed catch of three carp and three tench in an all-nighter.

Len gently returns a 19lb. 2oz. mirror carp to an Essex pit after capturing it on a boiled bait. The fish was the star catch in a bag of carp and tench that he took in one of the popular Action Reply series that starts on Page 66.

PICTURES: JOHN HOLDEN

On Top of the World!

The 1985 World Coarse Fishing Championship will go down in history as the one in which England's international matchmen finally got it right after years of disappointing near-misses.

Our lads took the world team title on the River Arno, in Italy — just one point ahead of the "locals" — and, next day, scored a double-top when Dave Roper, from Preston, finished brilliantly to become world individual champion, thanks to a 4lb. carp taken in the last phase of the match.

Due to a drought, the River Arno was 7ft. below normal for the teams' event and the flat calm produced in the glassy surface this perfect mirror image of the competing national flags.

Competitors and spectators line the banks of the River Arno, where the host Italian team started hot favourites but were outfished by England's aces, who relied on a long-range waggler float approach that made them the first side to win on running line, against the usual Continental pole tackle.

England's team plan centred on catching chub before temperatures soaring into the 90s put the fish off. But a delayed start meant that the chub refused to feed. So most of the team caught small catfish, similar to this one displayed above by Ian Heaps, who nabbed 21 of them to finish second in his section.

On top of the world, at last! The jubilant England team on the victory rostrum after their first team success at the highest level. Two section wins, two seconds and a 10th place gave them 16 penalty points, one fewer than Italy, who amassed 17.

PICTURES: RODNEY COLDRON

Increasing numbers of English coarse fishing fans have travelled abroad for holiday sport in recent years, with Denmark top of the pops. But Sweden could take over that No. 1 spot, judging by a recent trip to Haren Lake, 80 miles inland from the port of Gothenburg.

"The finest sport I've had anywhere", reports Colin Mitchell, of Angler's Mail, who was accompanied by photographer Rodney Coldron and guest angling journalist Don Bridgewood.

In just three hours Colin caught this 110lb. bag of bream on quivertipped maggots, including fish to 4lb. His account of Haren Lake's fishing delights is in page 24.

PICTURES: RODNEY COLDRON

Don Bridgewood samples first-hand the wonderful fishing that Sweden has to offer. He took catches of bream to over 100lb. and is seen here tackling another good specimen in Haren Lake.

TAKING TO THE BOATS

ALL ABOARD if you are thinking of joining the boat-fishing brigade for the first time! This specially-commissioned full-length feature is aimed at those who crave the deep-sea fishing thrills that lie beyond the blue horizon but have yet to step into a boat. Tackle ... baits ... clothing ... coping with sea sickness ... and choosing your first charter boat and skipper, are all covered in a comprehensive briefing.

by MIKE MILLMAN

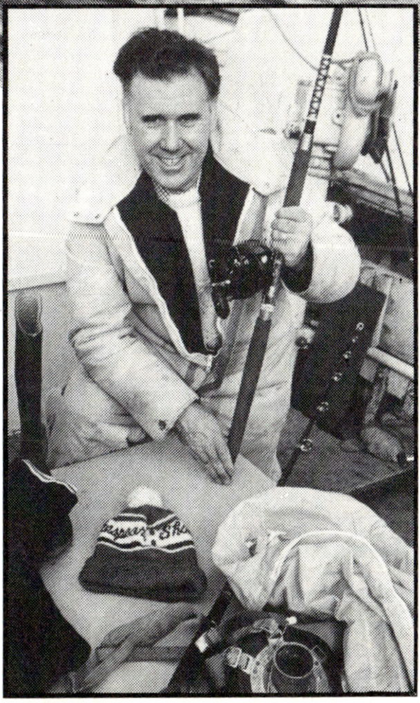

Mike Millman's selection of clothing for a boat angler, including a good quality buoyancy suit that will last for years and will help keep you warm, dry and comfortable when worn over several different layers of clothing. A woolly hat reduces heat loss through the head and thermal socks do the same job at the other end.

Starters

DEEP water sea fishing at distant wrecks or reef marks can be thrilling and rewarding, as thousands of regulars who return again and again with favourite charter can testify.

But it's not a game for the faint-hearted or for those who have not thought through carefully what it takes to be at sea for eight hours or more at marks which can be anything up to 20 miles from harbour — and in weather that can change dramatically in a short space of time.

Wet, cold and seasick anglers are likely to be among the first to drop out for good. But they could avoid those miseries and possibly get hooked for life by making a few basic, but essential, preparations before joining their first charter party.

Follow these guidelines and get your share of the excellent sport and good fellowship enjoyed by Britain's angling sailors.

HOW LONG? Always check beforehand with the boat skipper on probable length of the trip. It's not unknown for newcomers to set out for a day at sea, and even for an overnight charter, with inadequate clothing and no food or drink!

SEASICK? It takes only a moderate Force 4 wind to raise a nasty, choppy sea. And if it's blowing against the tide conditions can become downright rough. So make sure anti-seasick tablets are in your pocket. Some excellent drugs are available and if you fear sea sickness, or know you are vulnerable to it, take a dose before leaving harbour — don't leave it until out at sea.

CLOTHING must provide comfort and warmth, plus complete waterproofing with an effective barrier against the wind. Many dedicated boat anglers now wear buoyancy suits which, in an accident, can keep a victim afloat for a long period and slow down the onset of hypothermia, so buy the best quality garment you can afford and, with care, it will last for years.

Real warmth means thinking about the layers of clothing next to the skin. Thermal underwear is a "must", either Long Johns and vest, or an all-in-one combination. Then add a long-sleeved shirt with a warm collar, plus an oiled or waxed jumper (or three). Quilted, sleeveless body warmers, now available, are also very good.

Half-boots or wellies in a size larger than you normally wear will help circulation and allow thermal socks to be worn as essentials on colder days.

Loss of body heat is known to be greatest through the head, so choose a woollen hat with sufficient turndown to cover the ears. A cold angler is more likely to be seasick than a warm, comfortable one.

And put those waterproofs on before the boat leaves. It takes only one good slosh over the side to soak you and, once wet, you are more likely to become cold more quickly.

KEEP COOL. Boat trips are not always made in bad weather. I can remember many when suntan lotion has proved to be the most important item in my tackle. A brilliant sun reflecting off the waves leads more quickly to sunburn than on the shore. Windburn is another factor that makes lotion an essential.

A light linen hat, with a wide brim, keeps the head cool and body temperature down. And your feet need casual rubber-soled shoes which take up little room in a bag but can replace boots on hotter days.

WHICH BOAT? Choice of charter boat and skipper can be the most important decision affecting chances of a safe day of good sport — or a disastrous trip.

A charter boat and its skipper are licensed by an authority responsible for the sport where the craft is based. Their regulations require the boat to be inspected and the skipper tested on all aspects of seamanship and knowledge of the area he is working.

In law, sufficient buoyancy gear must be aboard for the maximum number of people the craft is licensed to carry. A licensing certificate is issued and this should be displayed prominently, usually in the wheelhouse. NEVER book a trip on an unlicensed boat — you could be putting your life at risk.

There are ground rules to follow when booking any charter trip. Study reports in the angling papers and identify those skippers who are consistently successful and know what they are doing. Follow up by referring to the adverts section.

Secretaries of saltwater clubs and tackle dealers at charter ports can also provide reliable information on the suitability of skippers and their boats.

Once you have selected boat and skipper book up well in advance as the more popular, successful skippers are normally very busy. Bookings at some ports are handled by an agency acting for the skipper, usually a leading tackle dealer who should be able to advise you.

But be warned — once a booking is made you have entered into a contract. If you fail to turn up the skipper can claim the agreed fee.

Tackle Check List

A NEWCOMER to boat fishing is faced with a bewildering choice of tackle. The best advice I can offer is to keep it simple and stick to middle of the road outfits, rather than specialised tackle. Only when you have become reasonably proficient should you consider paying out for more advanced rods, reels and other tackle.

That said, there are some excellent rods and reels on the market, these days, that will do the job very well and won't cost an arm and a leg to buy.

RODS

Most boat fishing requirements can be met with a rod of medium weight, which, roughly, means one in the 20-30lb range, capable of handling lines of a similar breaking strain. This should be adequate to deal with the type of fish you are likely to meet in the early days. As interest grows in specific types of fishing you can add other classes of rod.

Hollowglass or carbon are the only materials worth investing in; choose whichever your pocket can best afford.

Modern technological advances in the tackle trade mean that good quality carbon rods are now being produced at reasonable prices well within range of most pockets and represent a sound investment.

Most boat fishing rods designed for

Boat anglers carry a large assortment of tackle. This is Mike's deep-sea kit.

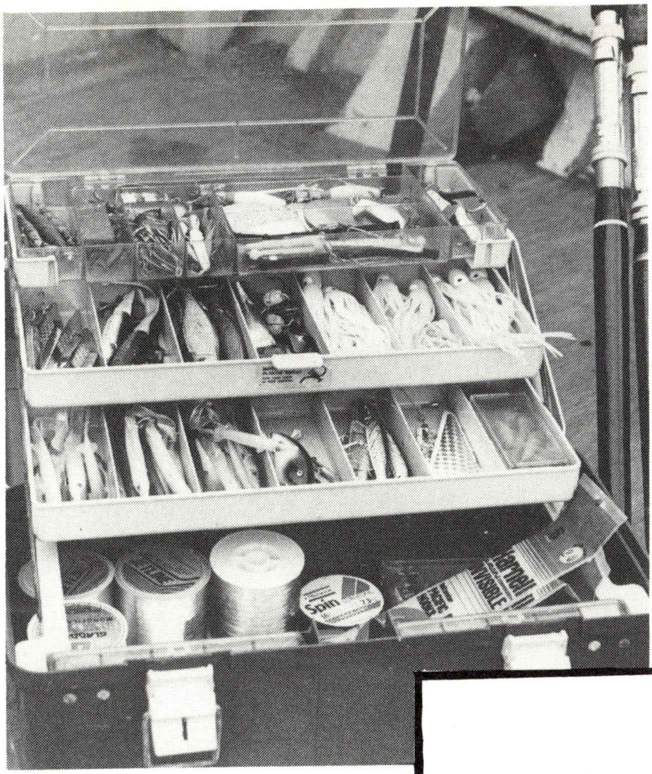

A large cantilever tackle box will hold a wide variety of tackle, ready to use.

deep-sea or wreck fishing are 7ft in length and usually made in one piece. Rods with ferrules or spigots should generally be avoided for the heavy duty work involved in this type of fishing.

A typical rod will have six lined rings, plus a tip guide ring, usually a roller which helps to reduce friction when line is retrieved under tension.

A boat rod takes a lot of punishment and you should make regular checks of rings and whippings for signs of wear. Replace any rings that are cracked or obviously faulty as these will fray the line and could lose the fish of a lifetime.

Wash the rod with warm soapy water after every trip to remove salt from the rings and reel seating and then dry thoroughly. Given this standard of care, a good boat rod will see you through many seasons.

REELS

The reel is usually attached to the rod by a heavily-chromed screw winch fitting and the butt and the fore-grip will probably be made from a material called Hyperlon, which gives a good grip even with wet or slimy hands. The reel seat should be well maintained and smeared with a film of Vaseline or thin oil to prevent corrosion and seizing up.

A good reel for boat-fishing will normally have a gear ratio of 3 to 1, so that every turn of the reel handle will retrieve three turns of line, which is adeqate in most practical situations.

A medium-sized multiplier reel is probably the most universal choice, taking at least 300 yards of 25lb nylon. Always buy the best reel you can afford as this is one area where it does not pay to economise.

Avoid multipliers with level winds, more commonly used in beach fishing, as these are not really suitable for tackling large fish at considerable depths.

LINES

Buy only monofilament line that has tremendous strength in relation to its diameter and presents minimum resistance to moving water. Braided nylon or Dacron are thick and at least twice the amount of lead is required to hold bottom when compared with mono. They are best ignored.

For starters, 25lb mono will be about right and there are plenty of reliable brands on the market. Most buy one brand and then stick to it throughout a fishing career, though there should always be room for experimenting if a particularly good make is available.

HOOKS

Hooks from 1/0 to 5/0 should be carried and checked regularly for sharpness and any distortion. Among the more popular models are Aberdeen, O'Shaughnessy and Kirby. Never return a wet hook to a box of unused ones because the whole lot will quickly rust and become useless. Either throw away a used hook — thoughtfully, please — or dry it thoroughly before adding it to the rest.

ACCESSORIES

As you become more proficient you will soon realise that a boat angler requires an amazing paraphanalia of accessories. Swivels of every size, snap swivels, links, running plastic and wire booms and coloured beads are always needed, along with a good range of lead weights.

Start off with a minimum and build up gradually as you become aware of your needs. Rushing out and buying haphazardly means you may end up with items never used.

USEFUL KNOTS FOR BOAT ANGLERS

BLOOD KNOT
For connecting line to swivels and hooks. Put the line through eye, twist around itself at least four times, put end back into first twist and pull tight.

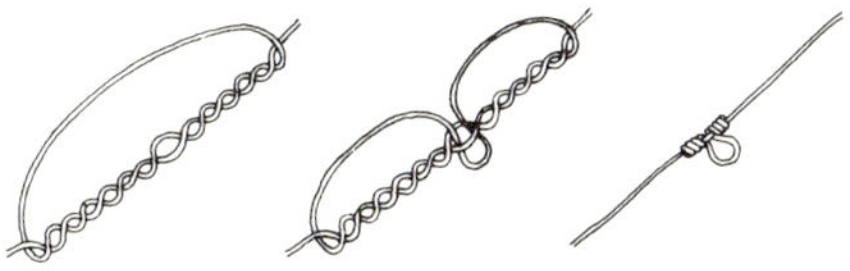

LOOP KNOT
Use when making up paternoster traces. A loop of line is taken from the main line and looped around itself. The middle of the loop is then pushed through the centre twisting, wet and pull tight.

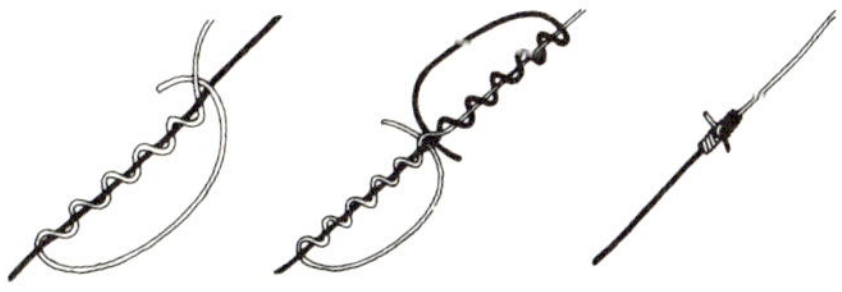

FULL BLOOD KNOT
For connecting two pieces of line together. Take one end, wind around opposing line and twict, take back through the first loop, do lho same with the free end as middle; wet and pull tight.

LEADS

Many new boat anglers don't appreciate the importance of using the correct shape of lead or sinker to hold bottom. Legering on the sea bed is best done with a circular grip and a range from 1oz to 1lb will be needed. Leads of the Arlesey bomb shape roll very easily in a tide run and are best used for on-the-bottom techniques, such as feathering for mackerel or drifting for pollack and coalfish.

Never drop down two leads together to make up a required weight. When tied together, the odd shape will be more easily dislodged by the tide flow and often makes it impossible to stay in the desired area and away from other anglers' lines.

FOR BEGINNERS IN THE DEEP END

Challenge of the Wrecks

A good conger comes aboard at a wreck mark off the Cornish coast

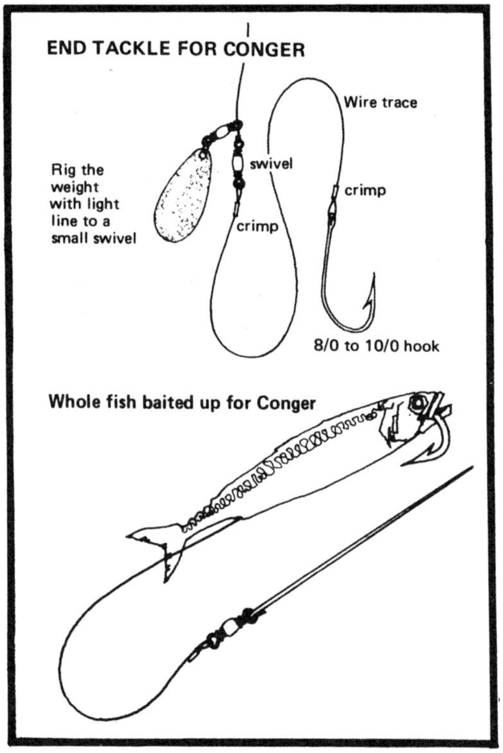

CONGER and ling rate high among the many worthwhile species available to Britain's boat anglers. These power-packed predators grow to impressive size. About 20 conger weighing more than 100lb have been captured by charter boats, with the British record currently standing at 109lb. 6oz. But much larger fish certainly exist, proved by two giants weighing more than 200lb. caught close to the coast by commercial boats.

Ling are more numerous, particularly at wrecks, and a catch of 1,000lb. by eight anglers in about five hours of actual fishing is not unusual. The rod-caught record is 57½lb., set off Stonehaven in Scotland, but the majority of ling taken at wrecks weigh between 15 and 30lb. and their voracious appetites mean they are not difficult to catch.

Both conger and ling are found very close to the seabed and baits are placed right on the bottom.

The well-equipped charter boat skipper has various electronic aids to help pinpoint a wreck or the best places on a reef and once the mark has shown on the graph-type sounder he manoeuvres the boat around to identify the exact spot where the baits must land.

Most skippers have detailed knowledge of marks they fish regularly and can find hotspots with great precision. So accurate are modern navigation aids that skippers can rely implicitly on the positional numbers which show on a Decca and similar equipment, so that the old system of first finding the general area of a wreck or a pinnacle, and then marking it with a buoy is no longer necessary.

Taking into account strength of tidal run and direction and speed of the wind, the skipper sets the anchor a long way uptide of the chosen spot. The boat wrecking skippers work hard at their job for conditions of tide alter, the boat must be re-positioned perhaps several times during the trip.

A 30lb. class rod and 4/0 multiplier loaded with 30-40lb. test monofilament suits most of the demands of conger and ling fishing. Both species have tough jaws and a strong trace is necessary. Here wire has given way to very heavy duty monofilament, which can be purchased at tackle shops by the metre or in 25-metre packs.

Using soft metal crimps which are squashed with flat-nosed pliers or a crimping tool, an excellent trace can be made up very quickly. It need not be longer than 18 inches. For ling the hook size is at least a 5/0 and for conger 8/0 to 10/0. A good strong swivel completes the trace.

A running boom which carries the weight is placed on the reel line and cushioned against the swivel knot with a small bead. A blood knot with a double turn around the swivel eye should be used.

To a great extent the feeding habits of conger and ling are different. Conger can display great caution and will "feel" and "taste" a bait before taking it down. This can last some time although wreck conger, which have competition for food, react much more decisively than those on a reef.

No attempt should be made to strike a conger until definite pulls are felt.

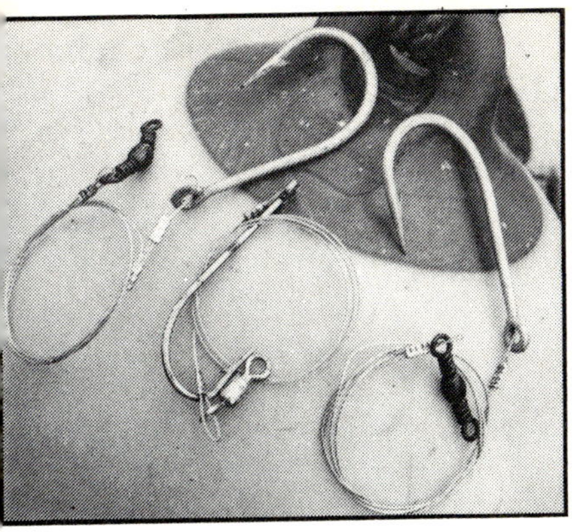

Conger and ling have powerful jaws so a wire trace, heavy duty swivel and hooks as large as 10/0 are needed.

The technique is to wind the slack line in slowly until the weight of the fish comes on the rod. Now is the time to set the hook with two or three swift sweeps of the rod, followed instantly by hard pumping to lift the fish away from the wreckage before it is aware what is happening.

The multiplier clutch is set just under the breaking strain of the reel line to ensure that the eel cannot gain ground easily. In the first seconds the advantage is with the angler and he must capitalise on it. Once the eel has been worked into safer water above the wreckage the clutch can be slackened to allow the fish to take line under pressure during the many attempts it will make to regain the bottom.

Bringing a large specimen that has not been played right out to the gaff is a sure way of losing it, so violent will be its surface fight. The importance of wearing a butt pad to gain more leverage on the rod during the encounter cannot be overstated.

There is a set of rules and procedure to follow when the conger finally arrives at the gunwale of a charter boat. The responsibility of getting the fish safely aboard rests with the skipper and he does not want to be crowded or restricted by a tight line between rod and fish so in the final seconds, the angler snaps the multiplier out of gear and controls the now free spool with a thumb at the same time stepping well back.

The conger is a dangerous fish and it is best to leave hook removal to the skipper. It is quite often left in the fish until the boat heads for home and for this reason the angler should carry at least six traces ready made up.

There is no delay between bite and strike when fishing for ling. So ravenous is the fish that the bait and hook will have been well taken by the time the attack registers on the rod tip.

A large ling is powerful and will attempt to head for cover the instant it feels the hook and line pressure. The safe water area above wreck or reef must be achieved, requiring a hard-set clutch and long, smooth, rythmic pumps.

Unlike the conger, the ling is affected by a swift change in water pressure as it is drawn upwards and most will suffer the "bends", as the stomach is forced up into the fish's mouth. As a result fish that are wound up quickly have little fight left at the halfway point in a depth of 30 fathoms.

Mackerel and squid are the most popular baits for both predators but the conger is a lot fussier and with the odd exception, will only go for food that is fresh.

A conger bait can be offered in a variety of ways. Usually a whole fish is mounted on the hook with the aid of a baiting needle which is pushed right through from mouth to tail. A small hook grasps the eye of the swivel and the trace pulled right through until the hook rests neatly in the bait fish's mouth.

A side of mackerel, or two fillets joined at the head or tail, are also first-rate conger baits, and will also do well with ling. A squid head often proves deadly and no self-respecting fish will refuse a helping of squid flesh. This is a durable bait and it is not unusual to catch several ling on the same piece.

Fishing on the Drift

NEARLY all the big wreck catches of pollack, coalfish and cod and to a lesser extent, ling are made by anglers fishing on the drift.

These fish stay very close to a hulk and the skipper must set up the boat so that it passes right over the hull or down its length. A species will quite often stay together on just one part of the wreck. Pollack swim high above it but a concentration of ling could be located well below the level of the superstructure and right on the sea bottom, which is also the case with conger.

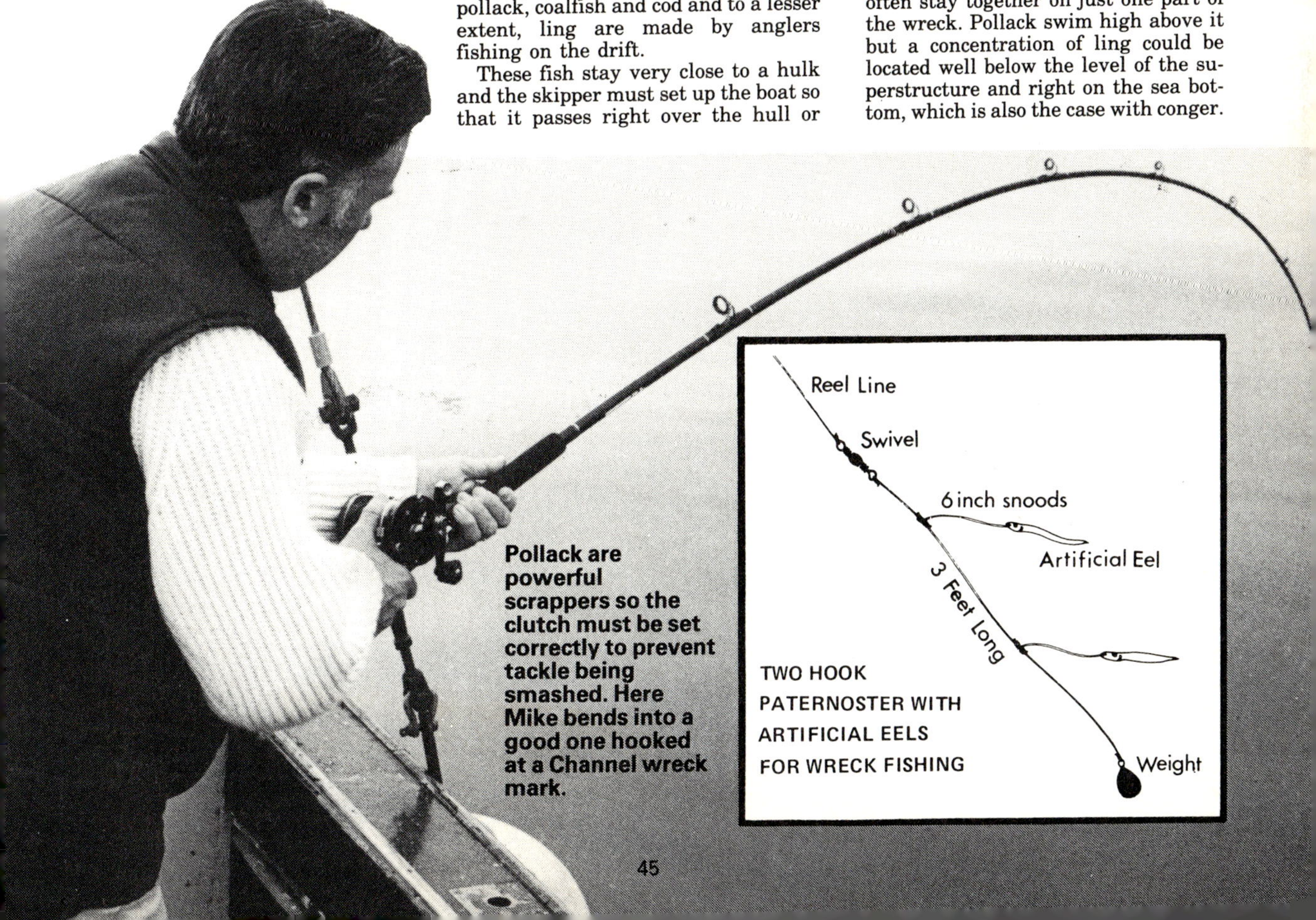

TWO HOOK PATERNOSTER WITH ARTIFICIAL EELS FOR WRECK FISHING

Pollack are powerful scrappers so the clutch must be set correctly to prevent tackle being smashed. Here Mike bends into a good one hooked at a Channel wreck mark.

Only rarely is drift fishing for conger successful.

Drift-fishing is hard work and if terminal gear losses are to remain within reasonable limits tackle must be under constant control. The snaggiest wrecks, which offer predators a rich source of small species to feed on, often yield the most exciting catches, but without a constant stream of directions from the skipper few fish would actually reach the surface.

A drift begins uptide of the hulk and once the boat's path is set the skipper's eyes never leave the echo sounder. He will already know the characteristics of the wreck from previous visits and a picture of the bottom builds up.

The height of wreckage above the bottom can be judged very accurately and as the boat approaches a high point, he will shout a warning. Some skippers are precise and will advise exactly how many feet the terminal gear must be lifted to avoid a hang-up. Old hands at the drift game respond quickly to instructions and lose very little tackle.

Fishing on the drift is at its best when the direction of wind and tide is the same. A crosswind situation can play havoc with the drift and, on such occasions, the dedicated skipper's lot is not a happy one. The boat moves sideways with the tidal run and if an average complement of 10 anglers is aboard only half the number can fish comfortably with lines streaming away from one side. That is why drifts are set so that each side gets a chance.

Pollack and coalfish are year round species on wrecks but the most exciting sport comes in the winter and the biggest specimens are taken in the period December to mid-March. Fish of 20lb and more are almost always females carrying roe which, in itself, can weigh 5lb.

Pollack are more numerous than coalfish, which is caught only rarely over rough ground, but pollack sport in those areas begins to improve in late April when the fish start to move back to the reefs after spending the winter in much deeper water, well offshore.

Pollack respond decisively to most artificial eels or pirks, with Redgills or Eddystone artificial eels accounting for most.

FLYING COLLAR RIG FOR POLLACK AND COALFISH

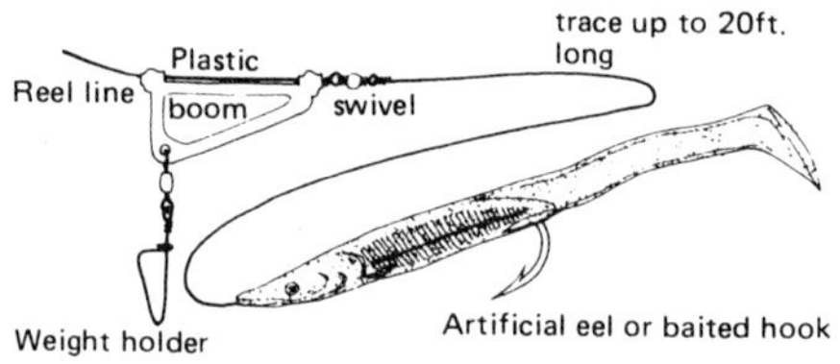

Sport hits a peak in late autumn when the fish can be expected much closer to the coast.

There are different terminal rigs for wreck and reef fishing. Pollack swimming over a wreck respond more decisively to a bait, artificial eel or a pirk. Most are taken with a size 177mm Eddystone or Redgill artificial eel, and colour can play a part in success. So carry a selection.

There are three basic ways of fishing for pollack and "coalies" at a wreck. The extremely popular "flying collar" is a boom, preferably made of wire, split-ringed and swivelled at all three points, which carries the reel line, trace, and a weight clip.

The trace is not less than 12ft and up to 20ft is used by many pollack specialists during fierce Spring tides which stream the monofilament and give the lure such devastating tail action. The technique is to let the weighted boom run to the bottom at speed with thumb controlling spool. Once there, a steady retrieve is begun, counting the reel turns.

Pollack always prefer a moving bait and after two or three fish have been caught the level at which they are feeding can be determined and valuable fishing time saved by moving quickly through the unproductive area.

There is no mistaking a pollack take! First comes tightening of the reel line and a slight curve of the rod, followed a second later by the line stripping from the reel which never fails to thrill.

The clutch must be set correctly for the strength of line and trace or the pollack will smash the tackle. Reel line is usually 18lb breaking strain with a trace slightly lighter.

Pollack are wonderful scrappers and even a 10 pounder will put in half-a-dozen searing runs. When it slows, line is steadily wound in. In a swift tide the fish will surface the length of the trace away and can be brought safely to the net hand over hand.

The flying collar trace, connected to a 4/0 hook, allows a natural bait to be fished attractively. A side of mackeral that is nicely cut, or a long thin strip of squid, rate as top bait offerings.

A less sporting method for wreck-fishing, but highly effective when big shoals are about, is a two-hook paternoster tied on a single length of heavy monofilament. The snoods carry artificial eels or a baited hook, with 4/0 to 8/0 being usual for specimen hunting.

The paternoster is weighted with a conventional lead or pirk and allowed to run to the wreck at speed. A predator will often make a slashing attack before the trace reaches the bottom.

It's not unusual to hook a couple of large fish at the same time! And that's a situation full of danger as the pollack immediately head off in different directions! The need for a very strong mono trace with well-tied knots is obvious.

A 30lb class rod is best suited for fishing to the multiple hook rig. Pirks take large pollack and "coalies" but a longer rod is needed with a fairly stiff action and plenty of butt.

Pirk fishing is tiring and the average man can't keep it up for more than half-an-hour. Pirks come in all shapes and sizes and you need to be equipped with weights of 20oz, 24oz and 26oz, when working deep water.

The flying collar is the leading technique for rough ground fishing and king ragworm often proves a much better bait than fish strip. This situation changes in the later months of the year when fish baits come into their own. The paternoster is a dead loss and a pirk also has no great merit for rough ground pollack.

When fishing over a reef the lighter your gear the better the end result will be. Reef pollack can display great caution and must be literally coaxed to take a bait or eel. A live sandeel is the best bait of all. Pass an Aberdeen hook through the lower lip of the eel and nick into the belly, just behind the head. A long trace is essential.

Cod Hunting!

The old saying "big bait, big fish," is never more true than for cod, which like a good mouthful.

COMMERCIAL trawling has drastically reduced the cod population and most of the spectacular rod and line catches now come from wrecks lying in very deep water in the middle of the English Channel. The area between Berry Head, in Devon, and the Channel Islands is the graveyard of several hundred wartime wrecks. Trips to these marks are mounted from Brixham and Plymouth and usually last for three days with a night stop in St. Peter Port, Guernsey.

This is specialist fishing and some groups go ashore only for a short time to purchase duty-free goods. There's a choice of sleeping acccommodation: a hammock strung between gunwales, or the hard deck! Even if this demands a high level of dedication the rewards in specimen fish terms are equally high.

In recent years the cod has become more of an all-year species in English Channel waters but no way can it be described as prolific at wrecks and reefs lying within 25 miles of the coast. An average 12 months will see about 300 fish brought back to the main charter fishing ports between Poole and Penzance. Few of those cod will weigh less than 12lb. and the majority are close to 20lb. backed by about a score in the 30lb. class. In the past two years seven cod above 40lb. have been taken at marks off Poole and Plymouth.

Apart from those specimens the figures do not take into account cod from the long-range Channel Island expeditions. In this category the top haul on a single tide is 53 fish weighing between 21 and 46lb.

Catches in Northern and Scottish waters are not what they were but there is still reasonable sport in the winter months.

Cod inhabit wrecks and rough ground and are also fond of hunting over a featureless bottom of mud and shingle. Their appetites embrace just about everything — including plastic cups! They are true bottom-dwellers — equipped with a long barbule, used to detect food that is lying buried and a hinged mouth that engulfs a big bait decisively.

A short leger rig with a single 6/0 hook takes many cod. The trace should be about 15in. long of 20lb. monofilament for reef and open ground work and 25lb for wreck fishing. In this context a cod is an equivalent species to the ling and it's best to use a heavy-duty mono trace connected to an 8/0 hook.

The terminal rig is carried to the bottom by a grip lead on a plastic carrier or a swivel with the lead tied with light nylon. This gives the advantage of a "rotten bottom" so that if the lead becomes wedged a sharp tug will free the trace.

The leger is basically a rig for fishing at anchor but when drift fishing the paternoster comes into its own. This is tied from at least 30lb. monofilament and carries two 6in. snoods and 6/0

Cod often attack the bait so fiercely that they hook themselves and the clutch must be set lightly to avoid the first rush.

A 30lb cod is an exceptional fish but Plymouth angler Paul Wilcocks really struck gold when he landed this pair at 35lb. 7oz. and 35lb. 3oz. from the Eddystone reef.

hooks, baited with mackerel, squid, peeler, soft back crab and all types of marine worms. The old saying of "big bait, big fish," is never more true than when applied to cod.

A paternoster arrives at the sea bed with the aid of a conventional bomb shape lead or a pirk which can also be baited. This rig is best suited to fishing on the drift but is also used with moderate success when the boat is at anchor.

Plastic or wire booms and three-way swivels have no part to play in a paternoster. An excellent trace can be produced very quickly from a 4ft. length of monofilament. A blood loop dropper knot is tied with a loop big enough to become the snood, which is placed through the eye of the hook with loop around the shank — actually tying it to the eye is unnecessary. If desired, the mono "boom" can be stiffened by making two or three overhand knots evenly along its length.

The blood loop dropper knot can be used to construct a single strand snood, which must be tied to the eye of the hook with a four-turn blood knot.

When drift fishing, the 20lb or 30lb class boat rod must be held. Once the paternoster has reached the bottom it is wound up so that the weight or pirk is just touching the ground. The rig is then raised and lowered gently which gives the baits an attractive movement. Set the multiplier clutch with just enough pressure to allow a good strike to be made, although this is generally unnecessary as the cod's attack is fierce enough to hook itself.

The technique of boat-casting is very effective for cod when working a muddy bottom which, more or less, is free of obstruction. Up-tiding, as it is also termed, requires a rod of at least 8ft and better if 10ft which can cast between 5oz. and 8oz.

The boat is at anchor and terminal gear is cast well uptide, using a lead with grip wires if the terminal rig is to remain in one place. Take care to brake the reel spool the instant that the lead hits water and then allow sufficient line to go off so that the bottom is reached. Once there, slack line is wound in, which set the lead's grip wires firmly into the mud or shingle.

Experienced uptide fishermen know the value of a "shock leader" which minimises the risk of terminal tackle snapping free as it leaves the rod — 30lb.-35lb. breaking strain is about right.

What is termed a rolling leger allows a great deal more ground to be searched. This technique differs only in the respect that a conventional bomb-type lead replaces the grip wires/weight with the run of water carrying baited hooks back towards the boat, usually in an arc.

It should be clearly understood that any form of casting from a crowded charter boat is potentially dangerous and the skipper's permission must be obtained. Some skippers outlaw it completely, particularly those based at West Country ports.

"Uptiding" has its origins in the shallow waters of the East Coast and is extremely popular and effective for cod and whiting off ports like Lowestoft.

Leading tackle makers now offer uptide rods in a number of categories, principally to cast 4-6oz and 6-8oz. The ideal "uptider" is at least 9ft long and carries seven lined rings, plus the tip.

Lightness and sensitivity, allied to power in the butt and a blank long enough to give complete control as the baits search the sea bottom, are the criteria. This type of rod is available in hollowglass and carbon fibre and the latter has a much firmer action.

Reef Fishing for Bass

Hooking and landing a double-figure bass is the angling thrill of a lifetime, as this lucky young angler found out.

BASS are the most prized of all the fish found in British waters and rated as worthy adversaries at the highest level of saltwater sport. But they have a very slow growth rate. A 10-pounder has roamed the seas for at least 10 years and can take another decade to gain a further 5lb.

Just how big they can grow is not known for sure. Marine scientists believe 30-pounders exist but Britain's rod-caught record is 18lbs 6oz, set in 1975 at the Eddystone reef, nine miles south of Cornwall's Rame Head and regarded as the bass angler's Mecca.

It is a tragedy that commercial fishing pressure on bass has reduced the population in the English Channel to a fraction of what it was 10 years ago, with a consequent decline in rod and line catches.

Other highly-rated areas where large bass congregate include the Manacles Reef, just offshore from Coverack on Cornwall's Lizard peninsula and the exposed Wolf Rock Reef, nine miles from Land's End.

Fishing for reef bass at the highest level is very much a specialist sport. Most of the fish are taken by small groups of enthusiasts fishing from privately-owned craft but there are opportunities for charter boat trips from Plymouth, Looe and Falmouth.

Bass sport is tightly controlled by the tide with the big catches made during spring tides which occur at new and full moon periods.

Lashings of grub is the big attraction for bass on the reefs. Giant launce (sandeels), which can be more than a foot in length, begin to appear over the rocks in early April, followed closely by the predators.

In the ensuing sets of spring tides, armadas of boats jostle for position over the deep channels. Timing is critical and true bass men, who live and breathe for the species, leave port at around 3 a.m. to be over the reef as dawn breaks. The first two hours are usually the most productive and, at times, it is not unusual for a score of fish, with a high percentage over 8lb, to be taken aboard.

Once at the reef some time is spent "feathering" for sandeel baits but the majority of anglers take their own supply, which is kept alive by a battery-operated air pump or by a flow of sea water into a fixed tank.

Live sandeel is easily the principal bait and outfishes all other offerings on the drift, which is the main method of fishing.

Some specialists fish alone and troll an artificial eel on a lead core line between the maze of rocks from a very long rod, which is held in the stern by a clip. When a bass strikes, the angler has to throw the engine out of gear, grab his rod and play the fish. Life and limb is risked but the few men who play this game believe the rewards of big bass justify it.

The normal tactic is to work the known productive channels with a follow-my-leader discipline. The boat is taken well uptide and drifted back along the chosen line, while a sandeel on a 3/0 Aberdeen hook, connected to a long trace, searches for a bass customer just a few feet above the bottom.

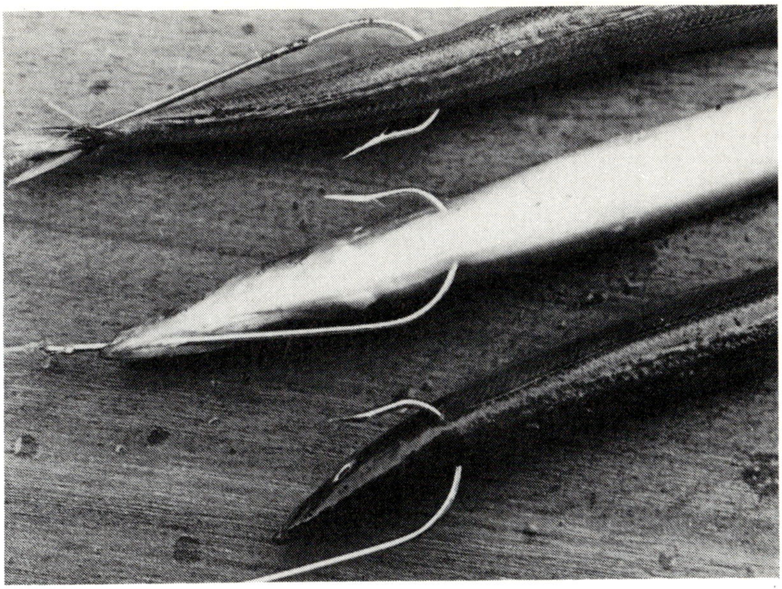

Live sandeel is the top bait for bass of all sizes but it is essential to use fine wire hooks, like the Aberdeen, to avoid damaging the eel.

Skippers maintain a gap of about 100 yards from the boat in front and once the drift is complete the boat is motored around in an arc to minimise propeller disturbance near the channel and the queue rejoined. On average, about 20 drifts can be completed before the fish go off feed. Late evening sessions can also produce a fair number.

The bass is a strong predator but best results come from using a medium-weight outfit. A rod of 7ft or more, with a lively tip action and a firm butt, is preferred and matched with a multiplier not bigger than 4/0, carrying 15-18lb monofilament line.

The trace is not heavier than 12lb and of a similar length, taken to the bottom by a ball weight of about 2oz which is placed on the reel line. A small bead is positioned between the lead and the trace swivel.

Possibly the most voracious fish in the sea, a bass makes a slashing attack on the sandeel or artificial, and its first run after taking the bait is extremely fast. This makes the rod buck violently and without a firm grasp and correct clutch setting, it can pop over the side like a cork out of a champagne bottle. That's why it is vitally important to set the star drag correctly so that line can go off under pressure.

Even a three-pounder will display amazing strength and agility as a true game species. But a double-figure specimen is a fishing thrill without equal.

Any patch of rough ground close to the English Channel coast or the Channel Islands is likely to produce quality bass. Sand bars, which usually occur in the estuaries of tidal rivers, can also be highly productive.

Marks with the biggest reputations include Teignmouth, Salcombe, the mouth of the Yealm near Newton Ferrers, in South Devon, and Cornwall's Fowey, Hayle and Padstow estuaries. Sandeel is the exclusive bait at all these places.

Most thinking anglers put back bass that weigh less than 2lb, but, unfortunately, a quay market price of £1 per pound is too much for some to resist. For this reason, conservation of the species must be a priority.

Tell the folks!

BEFORE you set off for a boat-fishing trip, make a point of leaving a note at home, giving details of the port from which you are leaving, name of charter skipper and his contact 'phone number, plus name of craft, if known. Jot down the approximate length of time you expect to be out at sea. This will help avoid unnecessary family anxiety when they check up, if your trip is delayed for any reason.

DIVISION ONE

The jubilant ABC team celebrate a 1985 Division One victory that came after "a little help from their friends"!

Division One Individual Champion Brian Oliver, a Northwich team member, with his 9lb 6¼oz tench bag, taken on a pole rig.

IT was an "inside job" all the way in the 1985 Division One National Championship when the Hertfordshire-based ABC team picked the brains of two local anglers in a move to win Britain's premier event on the Leeds-Liverpool Canal at Aintree.

ABC recruited Bob Wildman and Joe Burgess, who were not selected for their own sides, and their local knowledge of the canal helped put 712 points on the team card from peg 79.

That scoreline edged out Liverpool AS, the hot favourites, who totalled 701 from peg 72 and it also meant sweet revenge on Southport — who defeated ABC the year before on their home ground at the Grand Union Canal.

ABC's team plan was to let each man fish for himself but with a general approach of tackling the far side with pole and maggot, casters and squatts.

When the venue's famous tench went off the feed because of a sudden drop in temperature, the plan worked like a dream — producing only one section winner, John Price, but consistent points throughout.

In fact, the side were so confident of success that Mick Kelly, one of their star performers, decided to drop out on the day so that he could watch some of the team's newcomers.

Third were National stalwarts Barnsley with 696 points. Fancied scratchers St. Helens, Izaak Walton and Southport finished out of the running.

Individually, honours went to Northwich team man Brian Oliver, who was a 500-1 outsider but took 9lb 6¼oz of tench from a peg opposite a moored barge on "F" section, between Maghull and the Ducks Length.

Brian, 32, from Altrincham, lost more tench as they dived for cover under the barge.

DIVISION TWO

Local outfit favourites from Kirkstead came out top in Division Two on the River Witham but they were pushed close by Hyndburn and Blackburn AA.

SHEFFIELD baker Mick Hukin had never won even an Open match when he went into the 1985 Division Two Championships on the River Witham but his inexperience did not show as he cruised to victory from a pitch on the notorious "cyanide straight".

Apart from big match nerves, 37-year-old Mick, who was fishing from the Darnall Horticultural side, had to contend with the agony of a slipped disc which had laid him up for three days prior to the event.

Mick drew peg H57 (permanent peg 246) in an area he had not fished before. But the grapevine said it was a skimmer bet so he began by floatfishing down the middle and alternating worms, pinkies and casters on the hook to keep the shoal busy.

His first two casts brought fish but he had to ring the changes constantly in bait and methods to stay in touch. Feeding half-a-pint of hemp and 5lb of brown crumb into the swim, he took skimmers and roach, plus a bonus 3lb bream in the last hour and a half to finish with 13lb 14oz, almost 4lb more than the runner-up.

There were no surprises in the team stakes, when favourite Kirkstead finished top, but only by a weight decider. They were nearly beaten by Hyndburn and Blackburn AA, who amassed 734 points to equal Kirkstead's points total but fell short on weight at 29lb 13oz to Kirkstead's 35lb 3oz.

Eel fishing was the planned main line of attack for the Kirkstead team but, on the day, the eels refused to feed and that meant searching for "scale" fish to get vital points. Waggler fishing with big maggots brought the results and the rest is history.

CHAMPIONSHIPS

N.F.A DIVISIONAL CHAMPIONSHIPS

Date	Venue	Teams	Winners	Team weight lb	oz	dr		Individual highest weight lb	oz	dr
1906	R. Thames, Pangbourne	7	Boston	17	8	4	F. Beales (Boston)	4	11	0
1907	R. Witham, Kirkstead	13	Sheffield Amal.	21	12	12	A. Croft (Sheffield)	7	1	8
1908	North Level Drain, Tydd	13	Sheffield & Dist.	18	6	0	J. Mason (Sheffield)	12	2	0
1909	The Dyke, Newark	18	Leeds Amal.	7	5	4	J.H.R. Bazley (Leeds)	2	2	8
1910	R. Derwent, Hutton's Ambo	17	Leeds Amal.	5	8	12	A. Blackman (Hull)	2	13	8
1911	R. Severn, Kimpsey	19	Sheffield Amal.	53	6	0	W. Lowe (Sheffield)	13	4	0
1912	R. Ouse, Ely	20	Boston	25	9	0	G. Beales (Boston)	6	11	12
1913	R. Dee, Chester	22	Nottingham	2	15	0	W. Gough (Nottingham)	1	14	8
1914	R. Trent, Willington	20	Leeds Amal.	20	14	8	A. Skerratt (Derby)	6	15	12
1919	R. Ancholme, Brigg	24	Boston	20	0	8	T. Hill (Derby)	7	7	0
1920	R. Weaver, Hartford	29	County Palatine	12	4	0	R. Barlow (Hull)	3	1	0
1921	R. Trent, Burton Joyce	32	Derby	10	1	0	J. Wakesfield (Derby)	6	2	12
1922	R. Witham, Kirkstead	38	Lincoln	10	5	12	B. Hobday (Lincoln)	3	5	8
1923	R. Soar, Kegworth	41	County Palatine	18	11	0	J.W. Couldwell (Sheffield)	5	15	8
1924	R. Glen, Pinchbeck, Lincs	43	Castleford & Dist.	28	0	8	W.T. Willcocks (London)	21	8	8
1925	R. Severn, Worcester	46	Long Eaton	5	10	8	G. Allen (Provincial)	3	8	12
1926	R. Ouse, Naburn, Yorks.	47	Lincoln	23	11	9	A. Fletcher (Boston)	7	1	0
1927	Middle Level Drain, King's Lynn, Norfolk	47	Grimsby & Dist.	44	5	12	J.H.R. Bazley (Leeds)	16	5	8
1928	R. Severn, Tewkesbury	44	Leeds & Dist.	13	2	13	W. Tetley (Leeds)	3	13	3
1929	R. Witham, Kirkstead	44	Boston	50	4	0	J. Sykes (Boston)	10	15	0
1930	R. Soar, Kegworth, Derby	51	Sheffield Amal.	43	10	0	C. Muddimer (Leicester)	15	6	0
1931	South Forty Foot Drain	48	Hull Amal.	27	9	8	O. Daddy (Hull)	19	9	8
1932	R. Soar, Kegworth, Derby	47	Loughborough	24	15	0	H. Sallis (Long Eaton)	5	9	4
1933	R. Great Ouse, Olney, Bucks.	48	Sheffield & Dist.	33	6	4	Edgar Dabill (Sheffield)	13	15	9
1934	R. Thames, Abingdon, Berks.	54	Sheffield Amal.	14	3	11	H. Smith (Sheffield)	4	14	4
1935	R. Witham, Kirkstead, Lincs.	50	Lincoln	43	13	2	A. Kellett (Doncaster)	18	6	15
1936	R. Thurne, Potter Heigham	53	Lincoln	74	5	15	A.E. Bryant (Buckingham)	35	1	0
1937	Gloucester Canal	56	Groves & Whitnall	23	15	6	H. Jones (Co. Palatine)	9	9	9
1938	R. Great Ouse, Harrold	62	Hull & Dist.	38	12	7	G. Bright (Bristol)	21	13	8
1945	R. Trent, Newark, Notts.	57	Worksop	75	2	5	M.T. Cotteril (Worksop)	16	1	7
1946	R. Witham, Langrick, Notts.	66	Hull	57	0	12	G. Laybourne (York)	12	12	8
1947	R. Witham, Kirkstead, Lincs.	70	Worksop	57	8	4	W. Edwards (Rotherham)	9	4	8
1948	R. Huntspill, Somerset	72	Leeds Amal.	23	14	4	W. Thompson (Leeds)	14	9	12
1949	R. Thurne, Potter Heigham	77	Leeds Amal.	49	3	4	R. Woodhall (Whit. Reans)	15	6	8
1950	R. Nene, Peterborough	81	Peterborough	62	5	12	W. Rockley (Peterborough)	15	4	0
1951	R. Witham, Kirkstead, Lincs.	82	Doncaster	93	5	0	S. Buxton (Doncaster)	20	13	4
1952	R. Severn, Bridgnorth, Salop	88	Leeds Amal.	135	5	0	H. Seed (Leeds)	33	5	4
1953	R. Nene, Peterborough	92	Lincoln	72	5	0	N. Hazelwood (Cmb.)	27	14	0
1954	R. Trent, Gunthorpe, Notts.	98	Hull Angling Pres.	68	13	1	R. Lye (Notts. Fed.)	15	1	12
1955	R. Huntspill, Somerset	99	Sheffield Amal.	136	15	4	J. Carr (Sheffield Amal.)	68	2	4
1956	R. Witham, Kirkstead, Lincs.	94	Coventry & Dist.	86	4	4	C.R. Lusby (Lincoln)	25	8	0
1957	R. Severn, Bridgnorth, Salop	96	Notts. A.A.	22	8	1	H. Story (Notts. A.A.)	7	12	8
1958	R. Welland, Spalding, Lincs.	98	Coventry A.A.	59	15	4	W. Hughes (Northern A.A.)	24	3	0
1959	R. Nene, Peterborough	100	Bedford A.C.	86	1	4	J. Sharpe (Bedford)	57	8	8
1960	Rs. Ante, Bure, Thurne, Nflk.	101	King's Lynn A.A.	81	15	1	K. Smith (Norwich)	50	14	8
1961	R. Trent, Nottingham	103	Coventry A.A.	77	6	12	J. Blakey (Saltaire)	23	12	12
1962	R. Welland, Spalding, Lincs.	103	Lincoln	56	2	12	V.A. Baker (Derby Railway)	13	11	0
1963	Gloucester Canal	105	Northampton Nene A.C.	19	11	2	R. Sims (N. Som. & West Wilts.)	14	15	2
1964	R. Severn, Worcester	107	Kidderminster	50	13	2	G. Burch (Essex County)	32	3	0
1965	R. Huntspill, Somerset	110	Rugby Federation	93	7	8	D. Burr (Rugby)	76	9	0
1966	R. Witham, Lincs.	108	Boston	75	1	4	R. Jarvis (Boston)	29	1	8
1967	Relief Channel, Norfolk	111	Derby Railway	83	4	4	E. Townsin (Cambridge F.P.)	40	6	8
1968	Rs. Ante, Bure, Thurne, Nflk.	112	Leighton Buzzard	74	0	8	D. Groom (Leighton Buzzard)	36	6	0
1969	R. Trent, Nottingham	114	Stoke	32	8	2	R. Else (Lincoln)	9	7	3
1970	Middle Level Drain	113	Cambridge F.P.S.	97	2	0	B. Lakey (Cambridge)	35	4	8
1971	R. Severn, Stourport	116	Leicester	124	8	8	R. Harris (Peterborough)	40	5	0

CONTINUED ON NEXT PAGE

N.F.A DIVISIONAL CHAMPIONSHIPS

CONTINUED FROM PREVIOUS PAGE

Date	Venue	Teams	Winners	Team weight lb oz dr	Team points		Individual highest weight lb oz dr
1972	Div.1: Bristol Avon	79	Birmingham A.A.	51 1 12	248	P. Coles (Leicester)	33 8 0
	Div.2: R. Welland	81	Coleshill, Warks.	72 15 8	216	J. Hart (Whittlesey, Cambs.)	54 14 8
1973	Div.1: R. Witham	80	Grimsby A.S.A.	92 10 4	717	A. Wright (Derby Rly Inst.)	41 10 8
	Div.2: Gt. Ouse Relief Channel	92	Leigh & Dist. (Lancs.)	76 6 8	826	J. Wilkinson (Elthorne A.S., Hanwell)	43 1 8
1974	Div.1: R. Welland	80	Leicester A.S.	25 9 4	733	P. Anderson (Cambridge F.P.A.S.)	40 2 8
	Div.2: Avon (Warks.)	85	Stockport Fed.	71 0 8	1161	C. Hibbs (Leigh Miners)	47 3 8
1975	Div.1: R. Nene	79	Birmingham A.A.	43 15 12	814	M. Hoad-Reddick (Rotherham U.A.F.)	63 7 0
	Div.2: R. Trent	71	Long Eaton Victoria A.S., Nottingham	60 6 4	735	A. Webber (Wigan)	16 2 8
	Div.3: R. Welland	42	Crawley A.S., Sussex	18 9 0	394	J. Garrett (GEC Marconi, Chelmsford)	24 8 0
1976	Div.1: R. Trent	79	Birmingham A.A.	53 14 4	776	N. Wells (Newark)	28 0 8
	Div.2: R. Witham	76	Izaak Walton (Preston) A.S.	34 14 8	783	P. Marks (Exeter)	12 11 8
	Div.3: R. Huntspill South and King's Sedgemoor Drains	80	London A.A.	47 6 4	693	D. Knox (Cheadle)	38 9 12
1977	Div.1: R. Welland	77	Coventry A.A.	25 15 4	755	R. Foster (Rotherham)	39 10 4
	Div.2: Gt. Ouse	72	Huntingdon A.S.	34 10 12	687	S. Yeomans (Reading)	24 3 0
	Div.3: R. Trent	90	Stratford upon Avon	30 9 0	881	C. Robinson (Barnet)	18 4 8
1978	Div.1: Bristol Avon	79	Coleshill & Dist. A.S.	84 11 8	790	D. Harris (Bradford City)	48 13 0
	Div.2: R. Trent	78	Nottingham A.A.	36 13 4	806	I. Carrier (Long Eaton)	10 5 8
	Div.3: R. Witham	74	Bathampton A.A.	33 13 4	712	L. Constable (Chatteris)	29 8 8
	Div.4: R. Huntspill South & King's Sedgemoor Drains	34	Swindon Talisman A.C.	30 1 0	353	B. Shepherd (Ramsey & Dist. A.C.)	56 2 0
1979	Div.1: Gt. Ouse and R. Cam	80	Barnsley	10 15 4	700	M. Cullen (Oxford & Dist.)	11 8 0
	Div.2: R. Witham	80	Bathampton A.A.	32 2 0	746	S. White (Leek & Morelands)	11 13 0
	Div.3: R. Welland and Coronation Channel	73	Swindon Talisman A.C.	56 1 8	769	P. Deacon (Welling & Dist.)	17 5 0
	Div.4: R. Trent	56	Marazion A.C.	79 12 8	571	G. Salisbury (Marazion A.C.)	34 6 0
1980	Div.1: R. Trent	80	Nottingham Fed.	93 5 12	883	P. Burrell (Essex County)	27 8 0
	Div.2: R. Witham	74	Oundle	33 10 8	735	D. Green (Boston)	46 0 0
	Div.3: R. Ancholme	68	Wisbech	42 1 0	664	A. Kelly (Kidsgrove)	13 1 8
	Div.4: Yorks. Ouse	52	Telford (Salop)	7 13 12	461	D. Hall (Stoke)	6 10 8
1981	Div.1: R. Ancholme	79	Essex County	19 7 0	714	D. Steer (CALPAC)	21 3 0
	Div.2: Leeds/Liverpool Canal	73	Southport D.A.A.	52 3 4	687	D. Sayce (Luton)	16 15 0
	Div.3: Oxford Canal	71	North Staffs.	23 15 8	741	B. Clampitt (L'head)	18 10 8
	Div.4: R. Thames	80	Lamb A.C.	53 4 4	764	P. Hamlyn (Maidstone Victory)	20 0 8
1982	Div.1: R. Huntspill South & King's Sedgemoor Drains	78	Rotherham	27 0 4	718	Alan Mayer (Stockport Fed.)	21 13 0
	Div.2: Bristol Avon	74	Swindon A.A.A.	45 4 4	648	Ted Bird (E. Lincs)	44 5 8
	Div.3: R. Trent	76	Bawtry A.C.	64 4 0	741	R. Moir (Hayes & Harlington A.S.)	27 15 8
	Div.4: Leeds-Liverpool Canal	78	Congleton A.C.	36 12 0	741	E. Townsin (Ely Sugar)	8 13 0
1983	Div.1: R. Trent	79	Nottingham Fed.	141 1 0	741	D. Howl (Atherstone)	42 9 6
	Div.2: Yorkshire Ouse	74	Redditch & Dist.	39 1 4	689	A. Whitehead (Winsford)	12 15 10
	Div.3: Oxford Canal	73	Northern A.A. (Blackburn Centre)	27 10 3	724	W. Pearce (Lamb A.C.)	9 10 1
	Div.4: R. Witham	89	Kirkstead A.C.	44 8 1	980	A. Curd (Rye & Dist.)	22 3 13
1984	Div.1: R. Nene	77	Coleshill and Dist. A.A.	39 1 4	672	C. Gregg (Worcester)	42 11 2
	Div.2: Grand Union Canal	78	Southport D.A.A.	42 2 0	873	C. Hibbs (Leigh and Dist.)	10 1 2
	Div.3: R. Trent	73	Catch Match	65 8 9	680	M. Day (Travellers)	43 7 13
	Div.4: R. Ancholme	96	Weybridge	16 13 4	990	R. Ayre (Pendle)	34 11 1
1985	Div.1: Leeds-Liverpool Canal	79	ABC	20 13 0	712	B. Oliver (Northwich)	9 6 4
	Div.2: R. Witham	79	Kirkstead	35 3 0	734	M. Hukin (Darnall)	13 14 0
	Div.3: R. Thames	78	Letchworth D.A.A.	84 2 0	833	M. O'Neill (Manchester)	60 6 0
	Div.4: R. Trent	75	Cove A.S.	58 13 0	691	I. Bristow (Derby)	32 5 0
	Div.5: R. Trent	43	Trevs A.S.	71 5 0	372	D. Weston (Royal Oak)	49 14 0

DIVISION THREE

A sound team plan and unbeatable draw saw Letchworth and District AA win the Division Three Championship National on the River Thames.

Manchester Federation's Mark O'Neill is all smiles after winning this impressive armful of "pots" as individual champion in Division Three.

BOOKMAKER Billy Knott, Jnr., was £3,000 out of pocket after the 1985 Division Three event when rank outsiders from Letchworth and District AA won easily on the River Thames at Oxford.

For once, Billy had decided to relax his £12 maximum each-way bet and allowed a punter to put £22 on the Letchworth side — but didn't realise they had done their homework so well.

Their tactics, plus the fact that team captain Charlie Abrahams drew the prime peg at number 78, end of the section, saw the team finish well ahead with 833 points.

Letchworth tackled the Thames just as they would at home on their local Great Ouse — casting well across with maggots on light gear. A cold, blustery wind caused difficulties for everyone, but perseverance paid-off and the Letchworth men scored good points even on the hard sections.

Trailing well behind with 717 points from peg 4 were Northants squad Wellingborough and District, who were relegated in 1984 and had team manager Gerald Andrews to thank for their successful rebuilding.

Manchester chef Mark O'Neill went against the rules of bream fishing by bombarding his clear peg with 10lb of cereal containing four pints of casters and two pints each of squatts and hemp. But his heavy tactics didn't put down the huge shoal in his swim and he went on to win his first National with 60lb. 6oz.

Mark, who fished for Manchester Federation, took bream to 5lb., plus a solitary chub on worm and caster "cocktails" on a quivertip with size 16 hook to 2½lb. line. His peg, D36 at Eynsham, didn't warm up for the first 30 minutes but after that it was all go for the full five hours.

DIVISION FOUR

The Cove AS team, from Hampshire, just missed promotion in 1984 but made sure in 1985 by winning the Division Four event on the River Trent.

IAN BRISTOW, a 25 year-old Derby chemist, had all the right formulas to win the Division Four individual championship on the River Trent.

He found himself at peg K3 — a "flier" — and by following the advice of Trent ace Don Slaymaker he took 32lb. 5oz.

Casting a maggot-packed block-end feeder three-quarters of the way across the river, Ian got a bite on his fourth chuck, a fish on the next — and after that didn't look back, netting chub to 2lb., plus roach, perch and skimmers.

Seven pints of maggots went into the 6ft swim to hold the shoals and Ian, who is a member of the Soldiers and Sailors team, picked them off with white maggots on a 20 hook to a 1lb. length and 4lb. line.

Cove AS, from Hampshire, claimed the promotion they just missed the year before in the River Ancholme National. Their fine performance scored 691 points on a day when the Trent didn't live up to its reputation.

They were just nine points above runners-up, Brighouse, and were led from the top by their captain, Dave Sweet, who finished seventh overall with a 15lb.-plus net from Crankley.

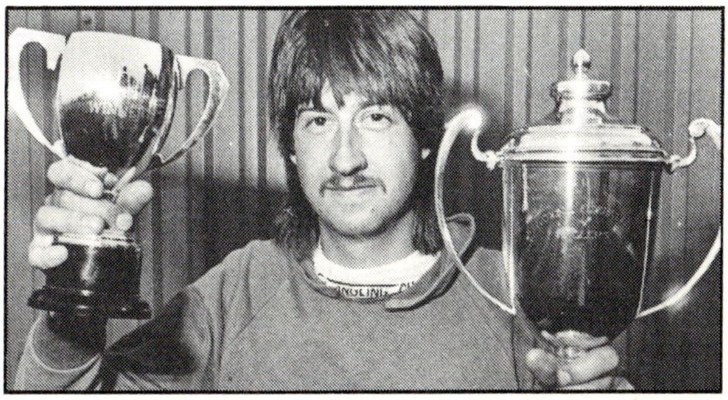

Derby chemist Ian Bristow followed the advice of Trent master Don Slaymaker and took the Division Four individual crown and these trophies.

DIVISION FIVE

Trevs AS, of Walthamstow, punch the air in delight after scooping the jackpot in the NFA's new Division Five.

THE National Federation extended their popular annual Championships in 1985 by organising a fifth division and that's where the bookies' favourites Trevs, of Walthamstow, beat 43 teams to win from peg 15 with 71lb. 5oz. on a River Trent that was in perfect trim.

Their victory was masterminded by skipper Dave Vincent, who was the team's top performer on the day, finishing fourth in the individual stakes.

Dave's plan was to adopt a tactical approach if they drew one of the fancied low number pegs but an influx of mid-week floodwater changed their plans to a target weight of 3lb. a man.

At the start, the team felt so confident of success that skipper Dave advised them to do their own thing. And it certainly worked for although they ended with less weight than runners-up, Woking, they had good points with four members taking more than 40 section points each.

On the night before the match, Doug Weston, a 51 year-old joiner from Sale, Cheshire, counted his 63 match trophies and it must have been a lucky omen for, next day, he added the coveted Individual Championship Cup.

Doug, who fished for the Manchester side, Royal Oak, drew peg K42 on the Holme Marsh section, opposite Muskham Church, and shunned the usual swimfeeder rig to demolish his 515 rivals with a superb stick float display.

Fishing with caster on an 18 hook, to a 1.7lb. bottom, he weighed in 49lb. 14oz., — 15lb. clear of the runner-up.

Doug Weston, of the Royal Oak, Manchester, caught enough chub from the Holme Marsh section of the Trent to win the Division Five individual title and these trophies.

He may be only 12 years old but Christian Chesters, of Leicester, is now an old hand after winning these trophies in the 1985 National Junior Championship.

NATIONAL JUNIOR CHAMPIONSHIP

LEICESTER'S super-efficient juniors made short work of 707 other youngsters in both team and individual sections of the 1985 National Junior Championships on the River Trent.

Without detracting from the team effort, much of the limelight shone on Christian Chesters, 12, as the youngest-ever NFA Junior National winner.

England junior boss Roy Jeffrey advised Christian how to tackle his peg at the famous "Aquarium" swim, three pegs up from Cromwell Weir. And while a gale force wind was buffeting other competitors, the pint-sized champ was working his way to a total weight of 20lb 2oz of chub and skimmers.

Christian took his fish on the feeder, fished halfway across, with casters in twos or threes on a 16 hook and 2.6lb hooklength. Chub to 3lb came to the lad's net and he handled them like a veteran, using five pints of casters, two pints of hemp and a little groundbait to keep the shoal interested.

Even a headache that developed halfway through the match couldn't stop Christian from achieving one of his ambitions . . . the other is to fish for England!

LADIES NATIONAL CHAMPIONSHIPS

DENISE HUDGELL, of Calcot, in Berkshire, caught 19lb 13oz of barbel from a River Kennet hotspot to win the 1985 NFA Ladies Championship.

It was her third attempt at the title after failing to make the frame on her previous tries at Ashton Keynes gravel pit and the River Trent, but her peg on the Kennet's Upper Benyons section helped her into the record books.

The swim had already produced a top weight in a match on the previous weekend and had all the form. But Denise still had to coax out the barbel and she did it in style.

Casting a caster and hemp-packed swimfeeder into the swim she soon had the Kennet specimens interested, losing two and netting one in the first ten minutes.

The action didn't let up and Denise had a hectic few minutes after the final whistle when she had to land a fish hooked right on time. But she coped and finished with five barbel to 5lb and a 1lb roach.

Double celebrations were in order when it was learned that Denise's mother, Mrs. Eva Foster, had taken sixth place.

Merseysider Linda Cooke was second on her very first National with four barbel, five gudgeon and a roach for 15lb 9oz.

Denise Hudgell, the 1985 National Ladies Champion, with her winning catch of Kennet barbel.

Leicester Juniors — all potential Likely Lads — pose for a team picture after their National Championship triumph on the Trent.

Date	Venue	Teams	Winners	Team weight lb	oz	dr	Team points	Individual	Individual highest weight lb	oz	dr
1978	Leeds-Liverpool Canal	56	Stockport & Dist.	21	1	4	611	A. Hunt (Coventry)	8	4	0
1979	Warwickshire Avon	51	Bristol and West	33	2	8	491	G. Bennett (B'ham)	17	10	0
1980	R. Trent	70	Leicester A.S.	27	2	12	708	P. Matthews (Newark)	16	10	0
1981	Leeds-Liverpool Canal	60	Northern A.A.	13	0	0	655	M. Church (Long Eaton Vic.)	5	8	4
1982	R. Thames	60	Peterborough	48	15	11	647	D. Rose (Stratford-on-Avon)	13	5	0
1983	Suffolk Stour	46	Leicester A.A.	19	0	5	473	G. Robinson (Oxford DAA)	12	7	14
1984	Lancaster Canal	58	St. Helens A.A.	15	10	0	687	S. McKenna (Northern A.A.)	4	8	15
1985	R. Trent	59	Leicester A.S.	46	8	0	602	C. Chesters (Leicester)	20	2	0

RODNEY COLDRON reflects on the 1985 World Coarse Fishing Championships, held on the River Arno at Florence.

ENGLAND'S FINE WIN

Packed Italian supporters watch intently as Tom Pickering, of Barnsley Blacks, nets another River Arno fish at Florence, helping England to their first win in the World Championship series.

THEY say that a million tourists flock into Florence, in Italy, on every single day through the year but trying to find even a "local" who knew that this famous city was staging the 1985 World Coarse Fishing Championships on the River Arno looked impossible when I arrived to report and photograph the event for *Angler's Mail*.

The taxi driver didn't know, the hotel receptionist hadn't a clue and neither had the manager nor his assistant. But within the next 48 hours nobody with the slightest interest in the sport could have been unaware that after years of near-misses, England had finally landed the world crown — and, what's more, made it a magnificent "double" with the individual title as well.

True, our lads made it by only a single point. But it was enough to reduce our tough match stars to tears of happiness and relief.

I watched it all happen and reported, unashamedly, that the England team fished superbly, always giving the impression they were winners. But the start was worrying for them when it was delayed by an hour because the Irish team had sent some of their members to the wrong sections.

The hold-up was a bombshell as England had banked on a prompt 10a.m. start for an early assault on the River Arno's chub before the sweltering September heat put them off.

So the team, chosen by manager Dick Clegg, of Barnsley, had to sit and sweat it out for an hour, praying that the organisational boob would not wreck their chances.

But it must be said that in 10 years of covering World Championships for *Angler's Mail* I have yet to attend one that has been organised perfectly.

The 1981 event at Luddington, on the Warwickshire Avon, would easily have been the best, given decent weather. And the 1982 championship at Newry, in Northern Ireland, deserved good organisational marks. But instead of using those two events as an organisational yardstick, and trying to improve, the following three championships in Switzerland, Holland and Italy seemed to slip back.

Even with the superb Italian setting and weather, and a crowd estimated at around 20,000, the organisers failed to provide a drinks stall, a tackle stand, Press tent or even a toilet!

But the England lads — Bob Nudd (Essex County); Tom Pickering and Dennis White (Barnsley Blacks), Ian Heaps (now of Oundle); Kevin Ashurst (Leigh) — adjusted philosophically to the delay, even if Dennis White's comments were unprintable! Lancashire's Alan McAttee and Dave Roper were left out of the team on the day.

Right from the late 11a.m. start England put the Italian favourites under pressure with early catches on rod and reel and waggler float tactics against the Continental's pole rigs, and became the first side to win with running lines.

Each fish landed by an Italian got a huge FA Cup Final type cheer ... every specimen slipped into an English keepnet was met with a deadly hush. But when the match ended a Wembley roar went up for England that was more than fair enough.

Dave Roper was put into the World Individual Championship next day and did England proud in one of the most nail-biting finishes for years.

Dave was neck and neck with Italian Roberto Trabucco for most of the three match hours but in the closing phase Dave hooked a carp of around 4lb and when he landed it after a 10-minute scrap he knew the crown was his.

Dave became England's sixth individual world champion after Billy Lane (1963); Robin Harris (1969); Ian Heaps (1975); Dave Thomas (1981) and Kevin Ashurst (1982).

Roy Steade, managing director of Steadefast, the famous Sheffield tackle makers who sponsored the England team, wore his "lucky" shirt on the banks of the River Arno and spoke for all of us when he said: "I am very proud of the team because they tried so hard. When other teams were enjoying themselves the night before the match our lads were checking their tackle and getting an early night in bed!"

And so say all of us.

The River Arno was 7ft. below normal on world match day — a fact that increased worries for the Italians, who were rated hot favourites as the home team. Their fears were well founded when England went on to win by one point.

THE NEW WORLD RANKINGS

	Penalty points
ENGLAND	16
ITALY	17
BELGIUM	25
FRANCE	31
LUXEMBOURG	41
SAN MARINO	43
SWITZERLAND	46
HOLLAND	48
SWEDEN	55
WALES	56
HUNGARY	57
AUSTRIA	60
PORTUGAL	60
YUGOSLAVIA	61
U.S.A.	64
DENMARK	71
W. GERMANY	77
IRELAND	78
SCOTLAND	79
SPAIN	94
FINLAND	96
CZECHOSLOVAKIA	97
POLAND	99

THE FRENCH CARP CONNECTION!

Max Cottis, from Ilford, Essex, was the envy of English carpmen when he landed this 68½-pounder at Lake Cassien, in the south of France. It's far bigger than any carp ever caught in the UK but still 3½lb. short of Cassien's best.

Lake Cassien, in the Var region of France and close to the luxury holiday playgrounds on the Riviera, has attracted dozens of English specimen hunters since word got around of the fabulous carp fishing. Dozens more will take the long sea and road journey — a 2,000 miles round trip for Max. On the same trip he bagged another great specimen of 47lb. 3oz. but, so far, his 68½-pounder is the best by a British tripper.

● *More about Max's exploits at Lake Cassien in page 28.*

The quiet spawning ritual among bream is usually unseen by anglers, since it lacks the noisy exuberance of tench or carp. Norfolk specimen hunter John Wilson became one of the few to observe bream mating habits when he captured these dramatic pictures at a lake in the Wensum Valley.

Males and females then paired off, although some females had more than one male in attendance, in the process that ensures continuation of the species.

A small group of big fish, 8lb and upwards, collected in the shallows at the side of the lake, searching out a likely spawning site. Areas with branches or dead reeds are usually chosen to provide spawn with a safe anchorage.

John Wilson was later able to get a close-up of the spawn deposited by the fish — watched, seemingly, by a large and suspicious bream!

URES: JOHN WILSON

High pressure building up over the Azores is what our weathermen want to see when looking for a warm English summer. But angling journalist Trevor Housby sought pressure of a different kind when he went to Fayal, the largest island in the mid-Atlantic Azores group.

Trevor was in search of the big-game fish for which the Azores are justly famous but the results of his visit exceeded his wildest dreams. In eight days of sport, he landed eight marlin — three white and five blue — including a new European blue marlin record of 856lb.

His big chance came from the Bank of Condor, in the shadow of Pico Mountain, where he trolled large Kona head lures behind the Pescatur big-game boat, Rabao.

On the last day of his visit, Trevor hooked this blue marlin of between 250lb. — 300lb, which battled for 35 minutes. Untypically, it did not leap but stayed down deep until Trevor brought it to the boat.

PICTURES: TREVOR HOUSBY

What a finish! In the very last hour before packing for home, Trevor contacted this huge marlin which slammed into his bait like a train. The fight lasted for 1½ hours before the monster came to the side of the boat — to weigh-in, next day, as an 856lb. new European record.

No matter how skilled an angler may become, or how successfully dedicated to a single species as the years go by, a fondness for roach will always remain, often from childhood days when a few "tinies" helped to start another eager youngster on a lifetime of fishing.

This picture of a trio of handsome roach from Ardleigh Reservoir, near Colchester, in Essex, makes it easier to understand why the species are such favourites, with their bright silver scales, colourful red fins and eyes — plus an apparent willingness to have a go at any time of day when most other fish seem to have deserted a swim.

Small roach are surprisingly easy to catch on a variety of different baits but bigger specimens are a different proposition. Hours of effort and patience are often needed in the search for one over the magical 2lb. mark, such as this 2lb. 9oz. beauty from the Hampshire Avon, taken by Peter Collins of Shepperton, Middlesex.

All kinds of factors, often outside an angler's control, can combine to produce a red-letter day that is perfect for catching big roach. John Wilson, of Norwich, found everything just right on a trip to Norfolk's River Wensum and finished with this splendid bag.

PICTURES: KEVIN SMITH AND JOHN WILSON

Brown trout don't come much bigger than this 14½-pounder. It is the largest ever taken on rod and line in England and fell to Dave Wood, of Stoke Poges, during a boat session at the Queen Mother Reservoir, near Datchet, Berkshire.

Dave used a fly of his own creation, nicknamed "Flash Bang Wallop", and the huge trout hit hard enough to strip more than 80 yards of line in an initial rush for freedom.

In a fight that lasted close on 20 minutes, the fish towed Dave's boat some distance before the full power of rod and 10lb. leader had their effect.

Around 2lb. is more the normal size for brown trout caught in this country, as this beautifully-marked fish from Chew Valley, near Bristol, testifies. But the jaw marks — probably from a pike or a bigger trout — show that even a fish of this size is not safe from predators.

PICTURES: ANGLER'S MAIL LIBRARY AND RUSS SYMONS

Whitby is famous for catches of king-sized cod but more than a few eyebrows went up when onlookers at the North Yorkshire port saw Nottinghamshire miner John Biddulph stagger ashore with this 43½lb. heavyweight.

John caught the huge fish 25 miles out, from a wreck lying in the North Sea deeps. He took a five-minute tea break before swinging back into action and ended his day with more than 200lb.

PICTURE: DENNIS LINLEY

MASTER OF THE RIBBLE!

by JOHN DARLING

CHUB STILL FALL FOR 'CRUSTY' KEN

KEN TULLIS, of Preston, is 76 and reckons he has spent 30 years fishing the Lancashire River Ribble. But you would be really wide of the mark if you thought his enthusiasm for angling is waning.

True, he has given up matchfishing and no longer casts a line in the sea because bait is so hard to obtain. But, on the other hand, he loves sport with trout and salmon on the wild rivers of North Wales and the Lake District.

It's when, however, it comes to big bags of chub from the Ribble that Ken's skill is legendary.

His speciality is fishing with bread crust but on the bright winter's day that I joined him on the riverbank he was less than happy with his local bakery.

They were on strike and he had been forced to scout around for the injection-moulded stuff...on early closing day!

The Ribble rises in the Pennines and threads through both open moorland and industrial conurbations before reaching the sea near Southport, and it is so well-known to Ken that he has intimate knowledge of the various swims, salmon lies and little corners of special interest.

But despite the countless hours he has put in, the river still holds a few riddles for him. Like why the chub on the south side of a big bend are almost twice the size of those on the north side.

The river was a foot higher and flowing faster than Ken would have liked for fishing his favourite swim and the temperature had dropped three degrees overnight.

Not so much as a tremble came from the big-fish swim so we moved to one on the north side with a similar depth of about 3½ft. Here the chub were eager takers of crust and Ken was soon unhooking the first of the day with a tiny pair of long-nosed pliers he bought 50 years ago for 1s 2d (about 7p).

It wasn't a big chub. Neither were the subsequent dozen or so that couldn't resist his time-tested tactics. But, as he was later to say, "if we had caught 'em over yonder they would have been belters!"

Ken expects swift action after laying a carpet of groundbait. If nothing happens inside 20 minutes he moves elsewhere. But he concedes that the big ones are crafty.

With his soft rod and forceful strike he pulls hooked fish several feet upstream of the shoal before playing the catch.

"You've got to fetch 'em out quietly so that the big old chaps don't know what's going on", is his canny view.

Ken is very particular about his feed and makes it from three parts of ground bread with one part of maize to bind it. He flattens the balls so that they don't trundle off downstream and tells from the sound of them hitting the water whether they are of the correct consistency.

A ball should arrive with a good, solid 'plomp' rather than a tinny splash, he says. Too much water makes the feed go like pudding, which is equally useless.

He is convinced that crust is superior to flake. "With crust, the hook is always in the soft part of the bread which has never been squeezed. Flake tends to bind — but I like to fish crust with a lot of flake on it," he maintains. Even so, there are days when Ribble chub prefer flake to crust but curiously, cheesepaste is no longer as effective as it once was.

Chub have not always been a major feature of the Ribble. Fish stocks have been repeatedly wiped out by pollution but chub seem better able to withstand this industrial onslaught than the brown trout, salmon and roach for which the river was famous before the last war.

But tough though they are, the chub can't compete in size with their cousins from the warm South. The weather is much colder here and this is reflected in the growth-rate of the fish. Ken's best Ribble chub weighed just 1½oz off 6lb — a real belter in a river where a four-pounder is a monster. His best catch was 275lb in three sittings and he once caught 137lb in five hours, to win Radio Lancashire's Angler of the Year award.

Ken Tullis, Lancashire's 76 year-old master angler, can still account for a dozen handsome winter chub.

Ken's tackle is simple enough. His favourite rod is 10ft long, light, lissom and made of glass fibre. His one concession to advancing years is a sight-bob at the tip, which he has built up on the glass for a few inches with a whipping of silk, painted fluorescent orange with white bands. But the real secret is at his fingertips. He is brilliant at touch-legering, especially after a stroke five years ago that left him blind in one eye.

Ken's favourite winter tackle is easy enough to remember — all the sixes! Sixpound line straight through to a size 6 hook on a six-inch trail, with a six-inch lead link — but four swanshot on the link leger.

He stops the line by threading it twice through a bit of float rubber. A wooden bead, which came from an Indian table mat, slides on the line to take the lead link.

MATCH LESSONS

Ken fished three times for the All-England Team in the 1950's. "I reckon every angler should put in a few years' matchfishing," he claims. "You learn more in a day's match than from sitting on your bottom here all week."

He has fished in matches throughout the country, frequently winning big events, and just as often finishing high up in the frame.

Ken decided to pack up a little bit early so as to show me something special in an area that is steeped in history.

Our way back to the car passed through a farmyard. "See here," he said, showing me what looked like a cattle shed. There, behind calves and young heifers, the back wall of the shed was ornamented with a huge stone fireplace, pillars and stone-mullion windows. They were all that remained of a ruined monastery.

Did the monks, I wondered, fish for trout and salmon in the Ribble all those years ago, before their peaceful valley was rent by the Wars of the Roses?

Or had they preferred, like Ken Tullis, to go for the chub?

ACTION REPLAY

When well-known specimen hunters return to favourite swims and spill the personal beans about their fads and fancies in tackle, techniques and baits, there's a fair chance we'll all learn a new trick or two! That's why this selection from the ACTION REPLAY series, first published in Angler's Mail weekly, has been selected and adapted as a permanent reference in this edition of the Annual. We start at an Essex gravel pit, where the guest star is LEN HEAD, Suffolk's famous carp and tench action-man.

CARP AMONG THE TREE ROOTS

THIS is a typical Essex gravel pit and it has been particularly productive for me. My best carp here is a 27 lb 14 oz mirror which I landed last season and the best tench stands at 6 lb 5 oz.

I've made a 4am start intending to fish until nearly lunchtime. The weather's perfect, warm with some cloud cover and a steady south-westerly wind.

As can be seen, this swim calls for accurate casting. you must drop the bait within a foot of those islands. Two or three feet short reduces the chances of a bite. Because I'm fishing so near the islands I'm using stepped-up gear with 1¾ lb test curve rods and 11 lb line. That way I have a chance if I hook a big carp among the tree roots and other snags.

4am

The matching pair of rods on the left are Bruce and Walker "Green Dragons", 12ft. long 1¾ lb test curve carp rods, designed by myself and photographer John Holden. They have tremendous reserves of power depending on the part of the rod you're using. The rod on the right is a prototype I'm testing and I can't say much about it at the moment.

I'm using two matching Mitchell 300 reels, still the best on the market in my book, while the reel on the prototype rod is a new Penn model shortly to be marketed in this country. Only two rods will be in use at any one time so I don't break Water Authority rules.

My bite indicators are specially converted Optonics, incorporating an LED (light emitting diode) and adjustable, differentiating bleeps. The monkey climbers are specially made 1in. polystyrene balls with a Fuji ring line attachment, and I've made the needles from stainless steel radio aerials.

Pictures by JOHN HOLDEN.

I am baiting with Salmon Supreme boilies made by Richworth, both mini and standard varieties. This is only the second time I've tried this particular flavour but results are already impressive. I'll be feeding the mini-boilies and fishing the standard ones on the hook.

My reel line is 11 lb Sylcast with a short 15 lb Dacron hooklength. I'm using a "confidence" ring, incorporating a bolt and hair rig in one, modified slightly in my own way. The 1½ oz lead is attached by a split ring to a 6in. anti-tangle plastic tube. When a fish takes the bait it pulls the tube through the ring until it meets a stop at the end of the tube which sets the hook. This six inches of movement warns me when a tench is playing with a bait.

The hook is a size 6 Au Lion D'Or on wich I've crushed the barb and which is attached to the bait by a 1 lb Dacron hair using a baiting needle. The offset point of this hook seems to give greater hooking power.

First I must feed the swims. I'm fishing three during day — two hard up against the islands, and one on a gravel bar in between two of the islands. I've not done any prebaiting, so I'm going to have to give them a good helping of bait.

I'll catapult at least a dozen pouches of mini-boilies in each swim with about two dozen baits in each pouch. That means nearly 300 boilies for each swim and on top of that I'll introduce half-a-dozen of the larger size boilies as well.

You have to gather the fish round the dinner table! After the initial baiting, I'll put further helpings of bait into each swim as and when I think they need it, and depending on the number of fish I catch from them.

After 90 minutes I get my first bite of the morning, on the right hand prototype rod. The monkey climber gave a series of staccato jerks as the fish took the six inches of line before the lead hit the stop at the top of the plastic tube. Then a real "churner" developed with the reel backwinding like mad as the fish hooked itself and shot off.

I always fish with the bale arm of my reels closed, encouraging churners, and I knew from the bite that the hooked fish was a tench. Despite the heavy gear it was more than a couple of minutes before the fish came to the net which is quite a long time on 11 lb line.

I weighed it straight away and at 5lb 2oz I was well pleased. A 5 lb tench is still a good fish in my book.

5.30am

7.15am

This is more like it! I'm in on the centre rod and it feels like a big 'un. It was a typical carp bite on the bolt rig — two quick jerks and then the reel started to backwind like crazy. Where there are snags the only answer is to hold on hard and not give the carp any line, so I picked up the rod and then tried to walk the fish backwards.

If you are lucky the fish comes with you as you step backwards and it's a much more effective method than trying to pump it away from danger. Damn, it's snagged up on one of those tree roots! I must have given too much slack line.

What to do now? I'll slacken off momentarily and see if that will persuade the fish to swim free on its own. It's worked! The carp is free of the snag and I wind down hard on it to keep it well clear of those roots.

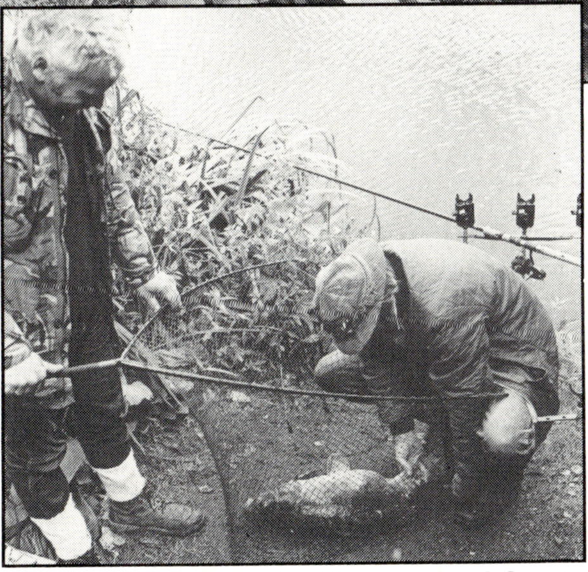

After five or six minutes, I get the upper hand. A mate of mine, Doug Wood, helps out to net the fish but once under the rod tip it makes a dash for freedom. I'm forced to give it line, almost for the first time during the fight. But it's beaten now and goes into the net first time.

I'm more than pleased with the mirror which goes 19 lb 2 oz, a good fish for this water. That landing net, incidentally, has 40in. arms, which is big enough to take anything that swims in British waters, and the mesh is knotless.

I use a slightly bigger mesh than usual because I find it easier to manage single-handed. The trend for micro-mesh results in nets that are very awkward to move in the water, particularly if you're fishing on your own and have to net your own fish.

11am

Let's have a cuppa, I think we've earned it! One of the nice things about carp fishing is the friendships you can build up and, as there are quite often periods of inactivity between fish, the kettle always seems to be on the go.

A 19 lb 2 oz mirror and 5 lb 2 oz tench in the same session can't be bad, and to round it off I take four more tench, none smaller than 3¼ lb before packing up at 11am.

The Richworth boilies have performed well and definitely deserve a longer run, though I understand that the fish tend to become wise to them fairly quickly.

I enjoyed today's session, though I usually fish for much longer periods, and usually at night. Night fishing allows you to be in place with the swims ready baited for daybreak which is why I prefer it.

7lb AN HOUR ON THE DERWENT

ACTION REPLAY is on the banks of the River Derwent in Derbyshire with Nottingham ace PETE WARREN and we're booked on the day-ticket stretch above the bridge at Borrowash. The famous County Council water which has seen so many huge match weights, is downstream below the bridge, but this section is still rated very highly. Pete is very confident of a big weight but as usual, the weather takes a hand...

THE wind is very strong today, almost gale force, and I've been looking for a sheltered swim. This one looks about right. The wind is blowing from behind, which should help me to loose-feed and it's coming from slightly upstream to help me control the float. The most likely-looking spot is on the far bank where the water is deeper, about 3½ to 4ft, and a bit quicker.

That's where I expect the chub to be and where I'll concentrate my main attack. This isn't the County Council stretch where all the big Opens are held, but it's still a very good water and I've had chub bags to 50 lb before, so I'm eager to tackle up and get fishing.

10.30am

ACTION REPLAY

Pictures by RODNEY COLDRON

AS I'm going to fish the far bank, I'll start on the waggler. It's a good chuck, about 30 yards, so I'll use a 2½ AAA model to reach the far side. The float is about 9 in. long and I've selected one with a black tip. The water is rippled on the far bank and is very light so that black stands out best; if there had been no ripple I would have used the more usual red or orange-topped version. I'll also set-up a stick float rig in case I can catch fish nearer in, with a black-topped version of my stick float made for me by Middy.

THE water is clear, despite recent heavy rain and that has decided my bait for the session. Mainly hemp and casters with three pints of each which should last for five hours.

I find casters are better than maggots here because maggots tend to be bothered by small fish. If the water was coloured I would rely on maggots as, for some reason, they work better than casters in coloured water and I've brought some along just in case.

I've also brought tares and sweetcorn but don't really expect to use them, though sometimes they will pick up the bigger fish. I mix my casters with the hemp because they are roughly as heavy as each other, which is important when feeding them into the swim.

I'VE tackled up with my favourite Middy carbon rod, couple with an ABU 507 closed-faced reel — the right-hand model because I'm left-handed. My main line is 2 lb Maxima, with 1.1 lb Maxima hooklength tied to a size 18 fine wire barbless Middy hook.

As you can see, I've shotted the waggler with a bulk shot, in this case an AAA, either side of the float to give me casting weight. Then there's a No. 8 shot, nine inches from the hook with two No. 4s between that and the float which is set to fish 3½ft deep, slightly overdepth.

I BEGIN by putting two or three pouchfuls of hemp and caster mix right across the river. On the second trot down I'm into my first fish of the day, a 10 oz chub which is a small sample for this stretch. I'm using only a 1.1 lb bottom but that's more than adequate to cope with any fish I'm likely to encounter today.

Chub aren't particularly hard fighters. Once you get their heads out of water they tend to give up.

As I expected, the fish are on the far bank line and I catch steadily for about two hours, with the odd better chub to 1½lb, plus occasional roach falling to my single and double caster hookbaits.

1pm

THIS chub is a good one for the Derwent. It's about 2 lb, while the average stamp is 1-1½ lb. That's probably because there are so many fish in the Derwent these days they are slightly stunted.

There are no dace in this stretch because the hordes of chub seem to have driven them out.

I've been catching steadily but the fish have been coming in spells when I've taken three or four and then nothing for a while. I think this is due to an influx of cold water from all the rain we've had. The fish are definitely not feeding as they should, even though I've been putting in a good pouchful of bait with nearly every cast.

TIME to try something a bit different to speed up the catch rate. So I've switched over to a stick float which takes four No. 4s spread out down the line, with a No. 8 nine inches from the hook.

I stop the float sliding down the line by putting a No.8 just under the float. Fishing the stick on a mid-river line means I can dispense with the catapult and feed by hand, which is more comfortable and much quicker.

After a couple of trots down, I start to hook chub two rodlengths out, along with odd roach and, surprisingly, one or two bream. I knew fish to 5lb had been taken in matches below the bridge, on the council water, but I didn't expect them to show today.

THIS inside line is going well now and I'm catching fish quite quickly. To build up a good weight on the Derwent means working up a good rhythm and I always try and bring my fish to hand rather than use a landing net, even if they are fish of 2lb or more.

This is much quicker and saves time messing about with the net and I don't seem to lose any more fish this way. Being left-handed doesn't prove to be a handicap in any way, even though most items of tackle are designed for right-handed use.

If I want to use a disgorger, for example, I've learned to slide it towards me to unhook a fish, rather than use it in the normal way. It all comes with practise.

I'M more than pleased with this 35 lb bag. At the end of five hours I would have been happy with 20 lb, given the conditions and the cold. The fish really came on well towards the end, on the inside stick float line, probably because I could feed more quickly by hand closer in.

Those bream were a bit of a surprise, though there are some good specimens in the Derwent. Why this is I can't say because, to me, the Derwent is a most unlikely bream river, being shallow and fast-flowing. Still, I was very pleased to catch them.

This river rarely lets me down, even in the worst conditions and I think I prefer it to the Trent for matches when the feeder, which is the dominant method on the Trent these days, is not allowed. But overall, the Trent is still my favourite river.

ACTION REPLAY

11am

This is just about the worst I have ever seen the River Wey in summer. Although it's a flash-flood river it's very unusual for it to be in this state in August. I think I shall be very lucky to catch a barbel, or anything else come to that. This is a swim I know well and I have had some excellent barbel from it — but it really does look impossible. There is a bit of a slack on the inside, though, which might just give the fish a little shelter out of the main current. If I'm going to catch anything that's where I think the fish will come from. So I might as well give it a go — but I'd much rather be in the pub!

Wading the Wey

ACTION REPLAY joins Twickenham schoolteacher Bill Rushmer on the banks of the River Wey, near Byfleet, Surrey, in a quest for a barbel or two. But the atrocious summer weather has again taken a hand and the river is a foot up, still rising, and the colour of strong chocolate. So Bill is not optimistic!

Pictures by KEVIN SMITH

My favourite rod — a 12ft. Bruce and Walker "Avon Perfection" which I bought secondhand and virtually rebuilt. It's irreplaceable as the only one I can find with a through-action and a test curve of 1lb. Most Avon-type through-action rods have a 1¼lb test curve which is too beefy for the light lines I usually prefer. When I bought it, the rod was ringed with Fujis put on the wrong way round. So I took tham all off and re-ringed it all the way through, but with more rings in the top section. That helps keep the line off the rod when it's wet and allows line to flow more freely. I'm using 4lb Sylcast which is heavier than I would normally use but think I'll need it in the strong flow.

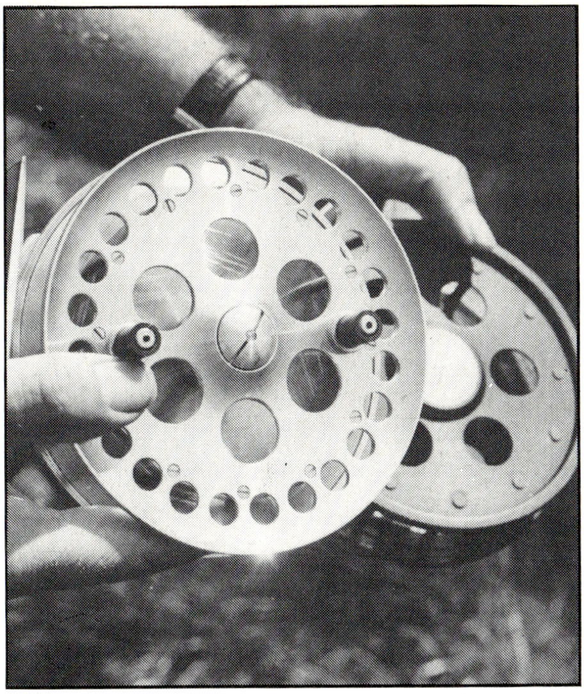

I've been using centre-pins for the last 27 years and I'm a great fan of them. The one in the foreground is a new Stanton model, made by Cliff Adcock, which I'm trying out for the first time today. It's a superb piece of machinery and very smooth. The other reel is one I have been using for the last four years, which I acquired from Hounslow Angling Centre and it's my personal favourite. I prefer centre-pins because they give better presentation when trotting and more control when playing big fish. I was first taught to use one by Jim Sharpe, whom I met on the banks of the Avon many years ago and who won the 1959 National Championships on the River Nene with a centre-pin. Since then I have used one for virtually all of my fishing and wouldn't be without it.

Flood conditions dictate which float to use today — it has to be a Topper Haskins-style crowquill Avon. I carry a range from 6BB up to 14BB and I have found them so useful for very swift-flowing water ever since they were recommended to me by Pete Melbourne of the Association of Barbel Enthusiasts. Three float rubbers must be used with this float, with one directly beneath the balsa body, otherwise it bends and cracks the crowquill and makes the float useless. My shotting pattern is very simple: I have bulked 6BB five feet below the float, which is set a foot overdepth in 6ft of water. Then three No 4s are strung out between that and the hook, a size 14 forged VMC, to hold any barbel or chub I may hook.

A bait dropper is probably the most essential item in my tackle today and vital to get bait to the bottom in the strong current before it is washed out of the swim. I've painted this one black to stop it flashing and scaring fish, and added weight to make sure it goes straight to the bottom. I use one a lot on the Avon and Kennet, which are very similar to the Wey in flood. Normally, I would use one in conjuction with a pole and 8lb line but I am using it today with my Avon rod. Bait is the hemp and caster combination which has proved deadly on most waters this year. I use it in a ratio of two of hemp to one of casters and I've brought four pints of hemp and two of casters in case I need to feed heavily.

As you can see, I have had to resort to chest waders to fish the swim as the floodwater is so bad. The waders give me more options than fishing from the bank and I can get far enough out to fish just the other side of that reedbed which is where the bank normally starts! This is where I expect the fish to be holed up and where I stand the best chance of hooking one. I started by putting in six bait-droppers of casters and hemp to lay a good carpet on the bottom. As they are quite heavy bait items they won't get washed out of the swim very quickly. I'll see how it goes before adding a further helping of bait. After fishing steadily for about an hour I have my first bite, from a chub of about 2lb, which fights well in the strong current. But it's not the fish I'm really after.

No wonder I'm smiling! This barbel of 2½lb is a turn up for the book under these conditions. It took the bait, two casters, as I held back hard against the current, and then it shot straight across to the far side of the river. Took me two or three minutes to land it, longer than I'd have expected, but understandable in these conditions I think. No more bites for a while so decided to scale down to 2.6lb line and a size 16 hook, with just one caster. That does the trick and I start to pick up chub, up to 2½lb, plus a roach of 8oz. I keep the bait going in at intervals, putting in four full bait-droppers at a time to ensure there is a good carpet on the bottom. But after a while the swim goes quiet; either the fish have moved off or some pike are on the prowl.

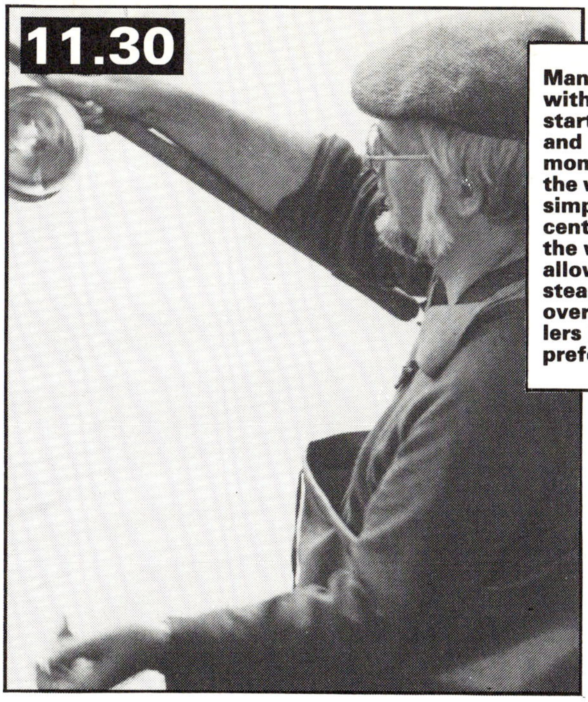

Many anglers complain they can't or don't know how to cast with a centre-pin but in my opinion it couldn't be easier. I start the reel revolving by pulling on line held in my left hand and then a simple upward swing takes the float out. The momentum of the float keeps the reel spinning until it hits the water when I stop the drum with my right thumb — dead simple! I retrieve by batting the reel which is why I prefer centre-pins without handles which, in my book, only get in the way. I have the line coming off the top of the reel which allows me to do two things — bat the reel away from me instead of into my stomach and stop the wind blowing line all over the place. I've noticed many southern centre-pin anglers have the line coming from the bottom of the reel but I prefer it my way, off the top.

I thought there were pike about and I've just landed one of 3lb which took a double caster bait. A few casts later and, blow me, a 2½lb pike grabs a small gudgeon I'm reeling in. There are obviously plenty of pike in the swim so I decide to fish deliberately for them. I wind 50 yards of 8lb line on to the centre-pin, attach a small polystyrene pilot float and then tie on a small wire trace. A small gudgeon, caught earlier, goes on to the treble hook. First trot down and the float disappears with a plop and I'm into a good fish! But after playing it for several minutes a large branch, brought down by the floodwater, snags the line and drags the fish into the bank where I can see it exhausted just below the surface. The only alternative is to strip off and go in after it as the water's too deep for my chest waders.

Success! Safely landed a 9lb 2oz pike. I hate the thought of leaving wire traces in fish so I didn't mind taking that unplanned dip in the river. Considering the conditions, and the fact that the river rose by nearly a foot while I was there, I'm very pleased with this little effort. The barbel I put straight back when I caught it as I'm a firm believer in not putting barbel in keepnets. At the end of the day, three pike, four chub and a roach represent a good day's sport — though, to be honest, it was hard work. If the river had been in a reasonable state I would have expected three or four barbel up to, say, 6-7lb from that swim but, nevertheless, I'm quite pleased with the results. Funnily enough, I had a pike of 6lb from the Thames at Sunbury the other day, and that took caster. Could be a new pike bait!

MAKING THE MOST OF THE SLIDER

Former World Champion IAN HEAPS teams up with artist TONY WHIELDON for an in-depth look at Ian's favourite float, the slider. One of England's leading experts with this method, Ian used it when he won the individual World Championship in Poland in 1975.

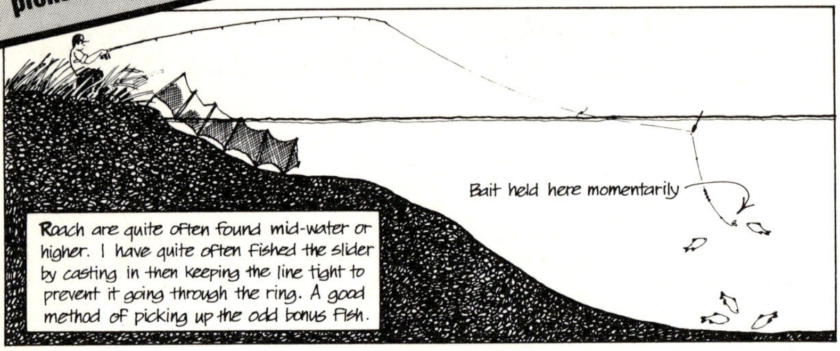

Roach are quite often found mid-water or higher. I have quite often fished the slider by casting in then keeping the line tight to prevent it going through the ring. A good method of picking up the odd bonus fish.

SLIDING floats can be one of the most deadly weapons in your float-box if used correctly — but sadly a lot of anglers just do not fish them any more.

I will always have a bit of a soft spot for this float as there was one on my line when I won the World Championships in Poland. Before that they always had a special place in my basket and there are still plenty of sliders of different shapes and sizes in there now.

The advent of pole fishing in this country saw us using the sliding float

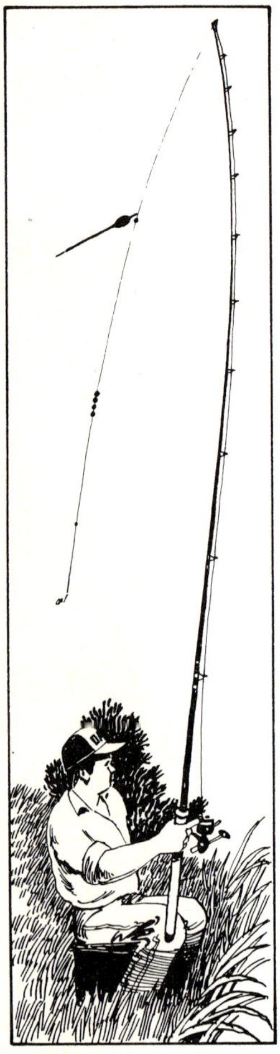
ALWAYS use an open-faced fixed spool reel when fishing the slider and, preferably, a 13 foot rod with a firm tip action.

Anti-tangle shotting

ALWAYS use an open-faced fixed spool reel when fishing the slider and, preferably, a 13ft. rod with a nice firm tip action.

The open-faced reel is needed because with the amount of line and distance at which you are fishing there is a requirement to pick up not just a fair weight, but also to bring it a good way.

With a closed face reel you would find the weight could bed the line on the spool and make things difficult when you go to recast, especially after landing a fair sized fish. An open-faced reel does not bed line and will also give you the extra working power needed to get the tackle in quickly.

A lengthy rod is required — I use a DAM Quickstick — because you need a fairly solid, sweeping strike to hit home the hook at not only distance, but also depth.

With the majority of lead around the float it is easier to cast and when you strike you hit the fish first rather than the float and locking shot. This means there is less chance of "bumping" a fish.

Main line should not really be below 2½ lb because of the casting weight and pressure you are putting on the tackle.

As in some legering when fishing at distance, it is possible to fish a shock leader of heavy line for punching out the float a greater distance. This need only be the length between the trace and back on to the reel for a few turns.

There are no hard and fast shotting patterns and as with any form of fishing it is best to experiment on the day. For a rough guide study my basic pattern.

The important things to look at here are the first No.4 shot which stops the float tangling with the bulk shot. That bulk shot is the workhorse that gets your bait down and pulls the line through the swivel eye on the float.

The shot below the bulk, the tell-tale, will give you the final indication when a fish takes the bait.

The distances I have marked are the ones that should give you fewer tangles but it may be necessary to vary them slightly to keep pace with the fish.

Casting is easy — overhead like you would with any waggler, but making sure that just before the float comes in to land, you check it so that the lead enters the water first and prevents tangles.

More often than not, it is best to cast the double ringed sliders under-arm so that the lead precedes the float. Casting overarm is possible but the tackle must be feathered down like the waggler to prevent tangles.

TWO RINGED BALS
mainly used for fast
river work.

Selected and adapted from features published in Angler's Mail.

By Ian Heaps and artist Tony Whieldon

less often as we were able to fish far greater depths without using one because of the sheer length of some poles.

But there are still occasions when we need distance and depth that the slider comes into its own.

There are two basic types of sliding float, one attached bottom-end only and the other which has two rings on its side so it can be fished in similar fashion to a sliding balsa float.

A lot of anglers make the mistake of believing that both types of float need a lot of lead on the line. They think that you need the big weights to pull the line through the rings to get the bait down to the fish, but this is not always the case.

Remember also, that just because you are fishing at depths of, say, up to 20ft with your sliding float, it doesn't mean there are no fish above that depth. Roach are quite often found at mid-water or higher and if you have a lot of lead on the line you don't stand a chance of picking up the odd bonus fish that are well off the bottom.

After you have cast, tighten to the float and close the bale arm. The bait then sinks slowly through the water as the float comes back up the line and if a fish takes your bait as it is dropping the float will lift.

This method allows you to cast to a number of places in your swim and fish at different depths. Try it every now and then to discover where the fish are and at what depth. You can alter your stop knot to the required depth when you find the fish.

Sliding floats are meant to help you fish depths in which you couldn't normally fish a fixed float — but always remember that like any other item of tackle we use, they are adaptable and can be fished in a multitude of ways.

There have even been times when I have fished a slider in just eight feet of water. Obviously, at that depth it would have been possible to fish a waggler or stick/balsa float but the slider on some of these occasions has let me cast from pegs where it was impossible to get other floats in the water because of obstacles, such as overhead trees, and also gives me a cleaner strike.

Easy to cast and control

THE two types of sliding floats — bottom-end only and two-ringed — are fished in completely different circumstances.

The bottom-end only float is basically for distance work or slow, deep water. The ringed balsa is mainly for faster river work.

Probably the most commonly used is the waggler bottom-end only type as many anglers find it easy to use. It casts easy, one eye means there is less likelihood of the line flipping back over itself and getting tangled, and when the float is in the water it is easy to control.

As I have said, I like my sliders, the big waggler types, to carry most of the lead in their bases. Also in this base is a tiny swivel through which the reel line passes.

The amount of lead in the float must make it stand up straight away so it is fishing for you immediately and it sinks bit by bit as the lead sinks through the depths.

By loading the float, it is possible to have a decent sized swivel — I use a 12 — and this means the float will not only fly through the air keeping pace with the shot, giving greater casting distance, but there will also be a good sized hole in the swivel for the line to slide through.

The main body of the float is peacock quill with a thin insert at the top of either thinner peacock, or bristle if the fish are very shy-biting. The body of the float, which carries the main weight and gives it stability, is made from balsa or cork.

The line is stopped from going through the bottom swivel's eye by using a stop-knot on the main line above the float. The idea is that the weight on the line pulls it through this eye until the knot stops it at the set depth.

Alternatively, you can now buy a line stop, a rubber grommett around 1/8" long shaped like a torpedo and which passes easily through rod rings.

It is very simple to plumb the depth. First find the correct shotting for the float so that only the tip will show. The tell-tale, your No.1 or BB shot, should make around one inch difference to how much the float sinks.

Cast the float out to a guessed depth and if only the tip is still showing it means the tell-tale is off the bottom. Now keep increasing the depth by 12 inches by moving your stop knot up the line.

Keep repeating this until more than the tip shows — which then means the tell-tale is on the bottom. Shallow off by six inches and now your bait will be on the bottom but the shot off.

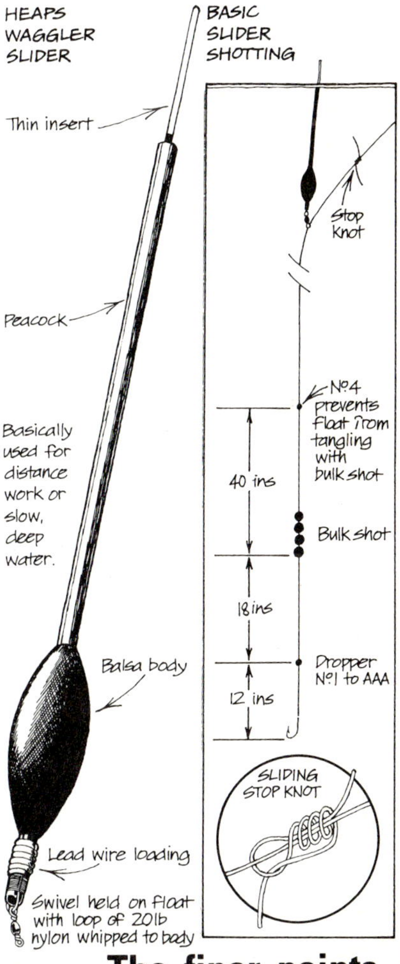

The finer points of swingtipping ▶

SWINGTIPPING

A fresh look at the almost forgotten art of swingtipping.

WATCH ANY OF THE TOP TIP ANGLERS AND THEY WILL HAVE THEIR RODS **STRAIGHT OUT** IN FRONT OF THEM.

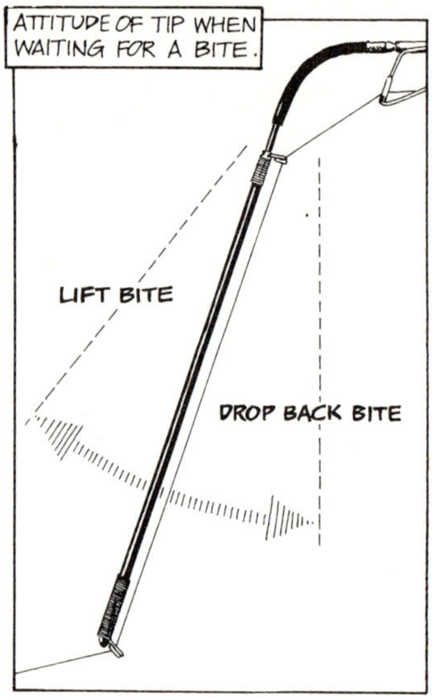

LINE UP THE TIP WITH AN EYE ON THE ROD — YOU WILL SEE ANY MOVEMENT MUCH MORE EASILY.

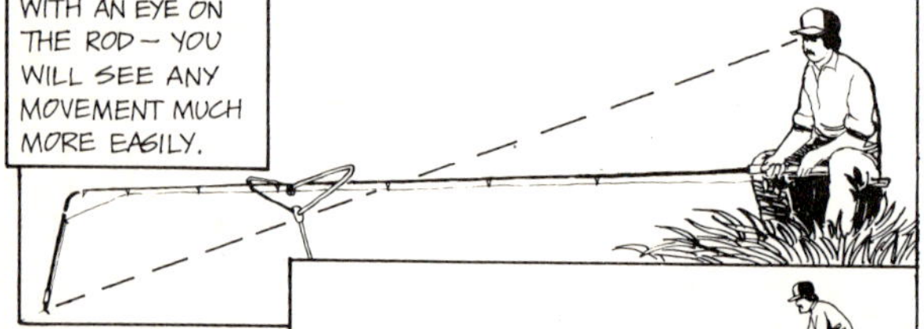

WHERE THE BANK SLOPES DOWN TO THE WATER, POSITION THE TIP JUST ABOVE THE SURFACE WILL GIVE YOU A GOOD BITE GUIDELINE.

SWINGTIPPING has become almost a forgotten method and for me that is a great shame as it can be a very satisfying way of fishing and a real killer when bites are hard to spot.

A lot of anglers are put off by the swingtip hanging loose at the end of their rods and they are frightened about casting, thinking, quite wrongly in most cases, that they could end up with a great tangled mess.

Swingtips are basically a stillwater tool, but even on lakes and ponds there is often a definite flow created by the wind and this has to be considered when choosing the length, weight and link of the tips.

Tips are screwed on to your rod with the standard thread that fits into the special end ring whipped on to most legering rods. From this screw there is a rubber link into which the tip itself fits.

These rubber links vary from a limp version which allows the tip to hang as if it were on straight flex, right through to specially moulded links which are pre-set at an angle. I prefer to use limp versions as they obviously register bites best. If conditions won't allow this I am not too keen on the moulded versions and these days would probably change to a quivertip.

In the past, some anglers — including me — used to weight their tips with things such as lead wire to counteract water tow or heavy winds but as far as I am concerned, tackle developments now mean this is definitely out. Stick to the strong links or change to a quiver!

The tips themselves can be made from glass, bicycle spokes, cane or, as I prefer, a piece of carbon which used to be the tip of a rod before it broke. Ideally, the swingtip should be around 15in. long. A six-inch tip can only move six inches, so the longer the tip the better the registration of a bite. Obviously, there are times when you can use a shorter tip, such as when fishing canals.

Bream anglers have always used fairly long tips because it gives the finicky species the chance to pick up the bait and move off with it without feeling any resistance.

SPOTTING THE BITES

A STRIKE STRAIGHT **UPWARDS** IS MUCH BETTER THAN SIDEWAYS — IT IS FAR MORE DIRECT.

MANY people I see fishing the swingtip, sit to the side of their rod thinking that this way they will see bites register much better. But watch any of the top tip anglers, and you will see that they have their rods pointing straight out in front of them.

SWINGTIPS ARE BASICALLY STILLWATER TOOLS, BUT EVEN ON LAKES AND PONDS THERE IS A DEFINITE FLOW, AND THIS HAS TO BE CONSIDERED WHEN CHOOSING THE LENGTH, WEIGHT AND LINK ON THE TIPS.

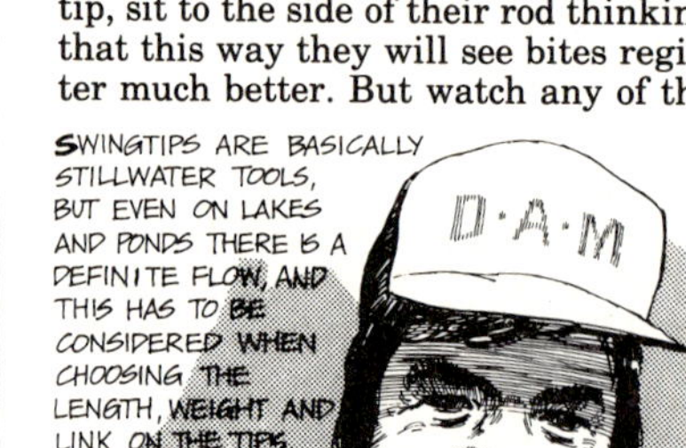

The idea here is that you must get used to seeing bites from behind the tip. A strike upwards is much better than sideways — it is far more direct.

If you can, line up the tip with an eye on the rod and you will see any movement much more easily. Should you be pegged on a spot sloping down to the water's edge, point the rod down over it with the tip poised so that it is just above the water which will give you another guideline as to when a fish has taken the bait.

Don't have the tip hanging down vertically from the rod top — always tighten up so it is half-cocked. This will enable you to see a drop back bite — that is when the fish moves towards you instead of away and the line goes slack.

– Great when the going is hard

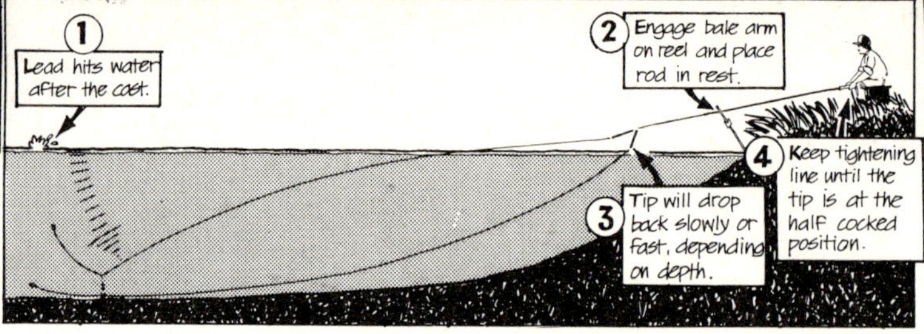

CAST OVERHEAD FROM STRAIGHT BEHIND YOU. DON'T POINT THE ROD AT THE WATER WHEN THE LEAD HAS GONE, KEEP IT ELEVATED.

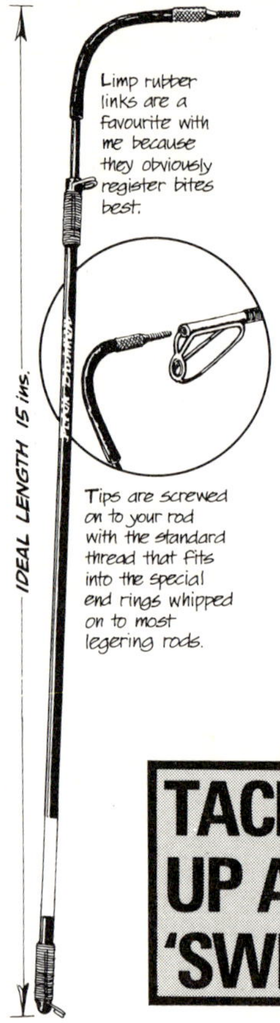

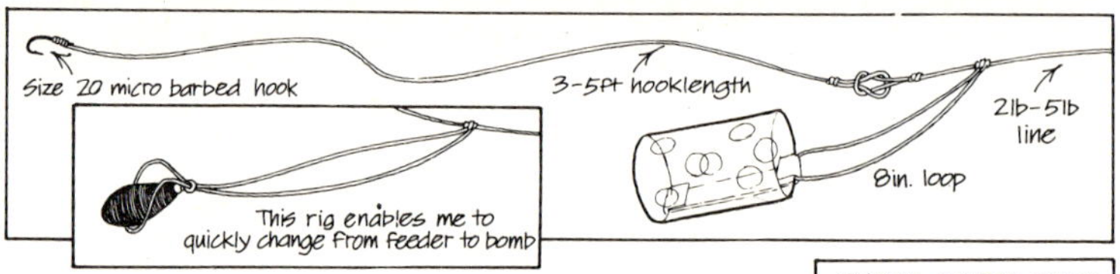

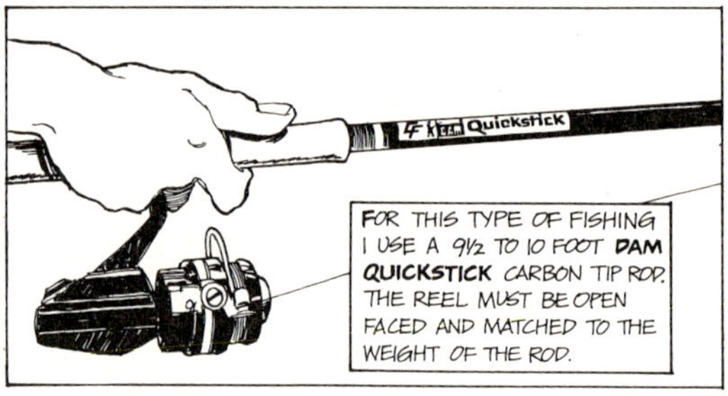

TACKLING UP A 'SWINGER'

After you have cast and the lead has hit the water, put the bale arm of the reel over and place the rod in the rest. The tip will be pulled out straight but will drop back slowly or fast, depending on the depth of the water. Keep tightening line until the tip is just at the half-cocked stage.

Always watch while this is happening just in case a fish takes. A falling tip may suddenly pull up or stop as a fish intercepts your bait. And, just as in floatfishing, watch for any unusual movements. When using a float, a second sense sometimes tells you that a shudder of the float or a slight falter while you are trotting is a bite.

When swingtipping in a breeze or with waves hitting your line, the tip may "freeze" or just pull that little bit extra. If you think it is a bite, strike! A lot of times a fish will be on. Sometimes one may have taken your bait and not moved off and when you start reeling in you are surprised to find a fish on the end.

CASTING with a swingtip isn't the easiest of jobs but there is no reason why it should deter you from fishing with it. Cast overhead from straight behind you, bringing the rod from six o'clock through to 12 o'clock.

Don't point the rod at the water when the lead has gone — keep the rod elevated. Surprisingly, a lot of the time you will be able to see the bomb, and as it is about to hit the water, feather the line down by putting your finger on to the spool of the reel. This will stop any extra line going out with a breeze and allows you to prevent bows forming and get the line from tip to bait tightened in the shortest possible time.

The choice of rod rest is important as there must be freedom for the line to run between the reel and end tackle to allow for tightening up. I use the Aquarian made by Keenets, which allows me to pull the line in continually so keeping the bait on the move — a foot at a time — which may induce a take.

For this type of fishing, I use a DAM Quickstick carbon tip rod. The ideal length is around 9½ to 10ft to give you power to cast distance but a fairly soft tip which allows you to fish light lines and still play out heavy fish.

Reels must be open faced and on this rod I use a DAM MV 30 or 40 which is matched to the weight of the rod. The bigger reel is needed for feeder fishing when you have to cast and retrieve a far greater weight.

Light legering means main lines of between 2 and 3 lb with 3-5 lb for feeder fishing. Remember to use as light a line as possible as this also prevents bows creating, and go for a line that sinks fast.

I tie my hook lengths before I get to the bankside and like them to be up to 5ft. long for when the fish are taking on the drop or when they are shy. The optimum length is normally around 3ft. and the bomb or feeder should be fished on a link around 8in. long.

My links are formed by making a loop in the main line above the hooklength. For feeder fishing, I prise open the lead clip on the end of the plastic body and then put the loop under the lead before folding it back. This enables me to quickly change from feeder to bomb simply by opening the lead strip and lifting out the loop to hold it in place.

Hooks should be as small as possible, remembering that bream to 5 lb are more often than not caught on 20 hooks rather than 16. The important thing to remember is to use a barbed hook, or one of the new very good micro barbed patterns on the market.

Often a big fish is played out on a barbless only to be lost at the net. The hook has made a slightly bigger hole over the long fight and there is no barb there to give you the extra holding power you need at the last moment when some slack line may occur.

Generally, I use a fine hook for roach and a small forged pattern for bream, remembering that soft baits like gozzers are best mounted on a finer hook so that they don't burst.

Basic principles of float shotting ▶

THE BASIC PRINCIPLES OF FLOAT SHOTTING

Shotting

IT IS well-known that correct shotting patterns can mean the difference between "bagging up" and catching a few bits, but that's not the only reason why they are fixed on the line with such precision.

Preventing tangles is another essential requirement. If you keep retrieving your tackle only to find the hook wrapped round the base of the float and the line in a hopeless knot, it's time to have a rethink.

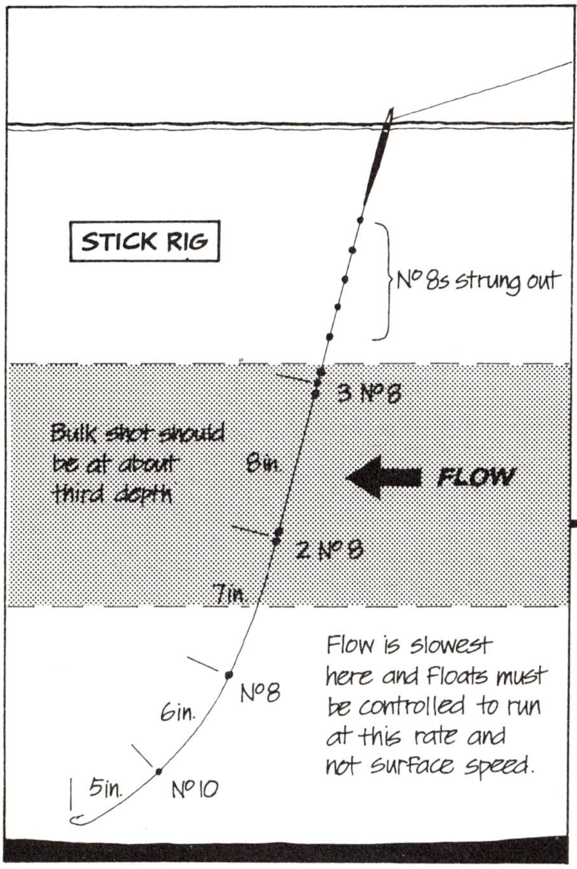

Correct spacing and choice of shot size are the overriding factors, and these are most easily explained if we look at a pole float rig.

Let's say the distance between the Olivette and the hook is 12in, then the tell-tale or dropper shot must go on the line below the halfway point or the hook could back tangle on the cast. That tell-tale should never be more than 5in from the hook.

This is even more important in running line floatfishing where more shots are employed down the line for control. In this case, the shots go up in size towards the float to eliminate tangles. The spacing rule applies more than ever, with the smallest space between hook and tell-tale and increasing towards the float.

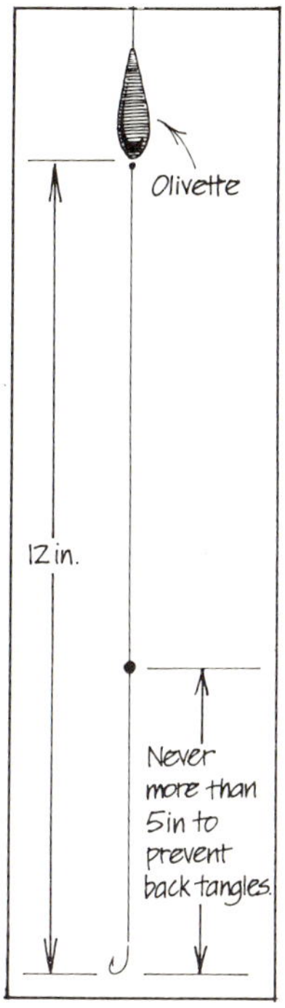

STICK FLOAT STYLES

STICK float fishing spawned the much-used terms "poker" and "shirt button" style shotting, which refer to the way the weight is distributed to ensure as near perfect bait presentation as possible.

The actual shot patterns remain similar regardless of depth and flow — it's just the shot sizes that increase to aid control. For example, a 6ft peg with steady flow may require No.8s whereas a deeper more powerful section would demand No.6s or No.4s.

If I were fishing a light stick with caster I would pinch a No.10 five inches from the hook as a tell-tale. Six inches above this goes a No.8 and seven inches above that two No.8 bunched together. Eight inches above these are my bulk shot comprising three No.8.

The bulk shot are crucial. I aim to control the float so that the line is tight to them. It is as though the shot form the end of the float — if we could use a float that long it would be ideal but it isn't practical.

Above the bulk I string five No.8 equally spaced or sometimes two No. 8 bunched above the bulk with three No.8s in a string. The latter pattern gives me extra weight, and therefore control, in the critical area.

The rig has to be held back to produce maximum bites and the bulk

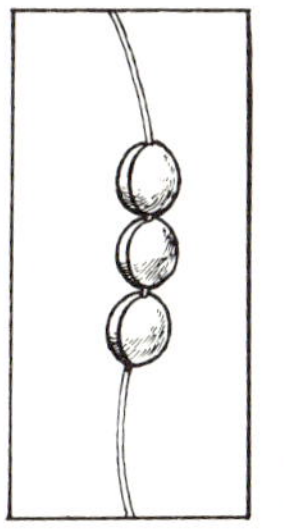

ALWAYS
Line up the splits in shots when bulking, to prevent line twist.

up for success

WAYS WITH WAGGLERS

SHOTTING a waggler is simpler than a stick but one rule must be followed — the majority of the shot go round the base of the float. Our aim is to transform the float into a form of throwing dart, to give maximum distance and accuracy.

In a swim 10-12ft deep, the "down the line" shotting would start with a No.10 near the hook followed by a No.8, two No.8 bunched and three No.8 bunched.

The bunched 8s could be substituted by a No.4 and a No.4 with an 8 and one No.8 but I prefer the linear outline made by small shot rather than a ball which may give resistance to current or wind.

The float is held or locked on the line with 3 AAA or one SSG and 1 AAA and cast with an overhead action to the desired spot.

I incline towards a straight float for most of my waggler work these days, believing that it offers less resistance to the strike and thus more bites are hit.

The rig I've described is at home on still and flowing waters. In shallow water I pick a float some six inches long and lock it with 3 BB. This is enough to take it down so just 3/8in is showing above the surface. The tip is trimmed down with a No.8 and two No.8 above that.

This set up is ideal for "on the drop" fishing but can also cope with bottom work and can beat drag if it is fished overdepth.

To slow up the bait a little, the bottom No.8 is moved down to rest on the bottom to act as a brake, and if the drag demands it the second No.8 can be split and slid down to join the bottom shot. By moving the float up and going up to 2-3ft overdepth, the rig can be slowed or stopped.

Never forget that water moves in strange ways and a correct shotting arrangement is often the way to overcome the prevailing conditions.

A perfect example of this came once when I was fishing the North Bank of the River Nene near the Dog-in-a-Doublet Sluice.

The flow went towards the big sluice gates and obviously, took my conventionally shotted waggler with it. But towards the bottom of the river it was a different story with the flow going upstream as the water backed up — taking my ground-bait along as well.

I got round this by fishing a slider with its heavy bulk shot down which gave the undertow something to grip on and the float actually travelled the opposite way to the upper flow. It sounds odd but caught me fish.

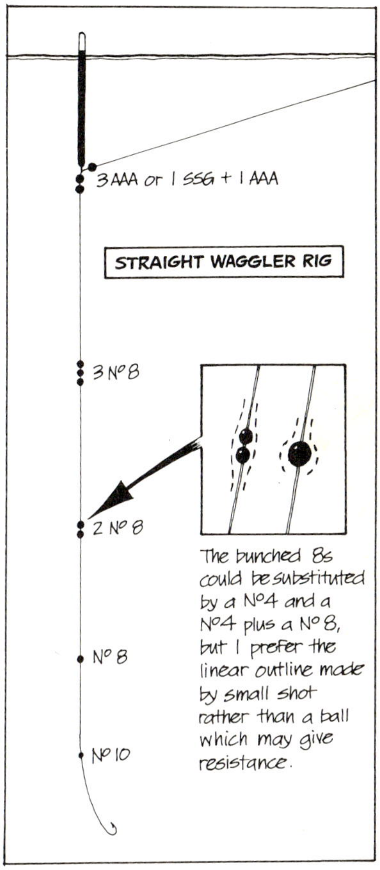

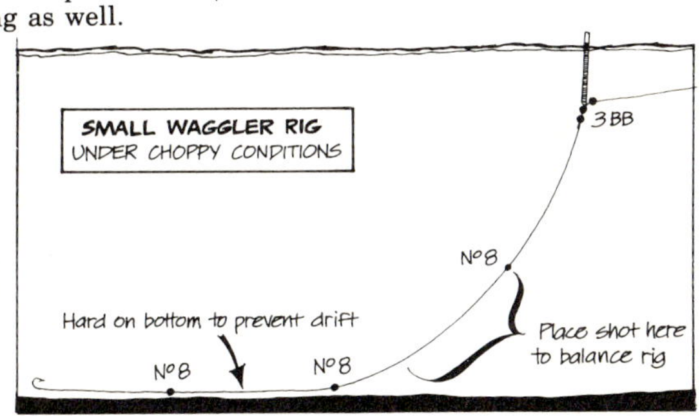

allows this to be done.

If the spacing of shot is correct, this pattern can be cast underhand — the preferred way — or overhead and feathered to land in a straight line hook first, without tangling.

Occasionally, I move the bulk shot up a little but this is rare. The alterations should be made to achieve the pattern I've described, not to break it up.

When maggot fishing with a stick, the fish tend to come up off the bottom to intercept the feed and here a light float shotted with a string of No.8s with a No.10 tell-tale is best. In most cases the float is run at the speed of the river so the bulk — with its facility to control the running speed — is not necessary.

A wire stem stick is better here because it gives a bit of extra weight for casting. In deeper and faster water the same spacing ratio applies and the bulk still falls onto the edge of the first and second third of the depth. The shots are bigger but if the current is faster still a balsa is the answer.

Shotting a balsa is a straightforward bulk and dropper — but remember to keep the dropper nearer the hook to avoid tangles. One other thing — always line up the splits in shots when bulking to prevent line spin.

One rule must be followed when shotting a waggler — the majority of the shot go round the base of the float.

Our aim is to transform the float into a form of throwing dart, to give distance and accuracy.

British Record Fish

FRESHWATER FISH

Recognised as at January 1986.

	Weight lb oz dr	kilogrms	Captor and Venue	Date
Barbel	13 12 0:	6 237	J. Day, Hampshire Avon	1962
Bleak	0 4 4:	0 120	B. Derrington, River Monnow, Mon.	1982
Bream (Common, Bronze)	13 12 0:	6 236	A. Smith, Oxfordshire gravel pit	1983
Bullhead (Millers Thumb)	0 1 0:	0 028	R. Johnson, Bramley/Shamley Green River, Surrey	1983
Carp	44 0 0:	19 957	R. Walker, Redmire Pool	1952
Carp, Crucian	5 10 8:	2 565	G. Halls, Lakes, Kings Lynn, Norfolk	1976
Carp, Grass	9 12 0:	4 422	G. W. Gwilt, Trawsfynnyd Lake, N. Wales	1983
Catfish (Wels)	43 8 0:	19 730	R. J. Bray, Wilstone Reservoir, Tring, Herts.	1970
Char	3 4 0:	1 480	S. C. Rex, Loch Dubhlochan, Inverness	1982
Chub	7 6 0:	3 345	W. L. Warren, Hampshire Avon	1957
Dace	1 4 4:	0 574	J. L. Gasson, Little Ouse, Thetford, Norfolk	1960
Eel	11 2 0:	5 046	S. Terry, Kingfisher Lake, Nr. Ringwood, Hants	1978
Grayling	3 10 0:	1 644	I. White, River Allen, Dorset	1983
Gudgeon	0 4 4:	0 120	M. J. Brown, Ebbw Vale, Gwent	1977
Minnow	0 0 13:	0 023	R. Merrifield, River Calder, Lancs.	1981
Orfe, Golden	4 3 8:	1 913	D. R. Charles, River Kennet, Berks.	1983
Perch	5 9 0:	2 523	J. Shayler, private Kent lake	1985
Pike	40 0 0:	18 143	P. D. Hancock, Horsey Mere, Norfolk	1967
Pike-perch (Walleye)	11 12 0:	5 329	F. Adams, Delph, Welney, Cambs.	1934
Pike-perch (Zander)	17 4 0:	7 824	D. Litton, Great Ouse Relief Channel	1977
Pollan	— — —:	— —	Open	
Pumpkinseed	0 2 10:	0 074	A. Baverstock, GLC Highgate Pond, London	1977
Roach	4 1 0:	1 824	R. G. Jones, Notts, gravel pit	1975
Rudd	4 8 0:	2 041	Rev. E.C. Alston, Thetford, Norfolk	1933
Ruffe	0 5 4:	0 148	R. J. Jenkins, West View Farm, Cumbria	1980
Salmon	64 0 0:	29 029	Miss G. W. Ballintyne, River Tay, Scotland	1922
Schelly (Skelly)	1 10 0:	0 737	W. Wainwright, Ullswater, Cumbria	1976
Tench	12 8 11:	5 689	A. Wilson, Wilstone Reservoir, Tring	1985
Trout, American Brook (Brook Char)	5 13 8:	2 650	A. Pearson, Avington Fishery, Hants.	1981
Trout, Brown	19 9 4:	8 880	A. Jackson, Loch Quoich, Inverness-shire	1978
Trout, Rainbow	19 8 0:	8 844	A. Pearson, Avington Fishery, Hants.	1977
Trout, Sea	20 0 0:	9 071	G. Leavy, River Tweed, Peebles, Scotland	1983
Vendace	— — —:	— —	Open	

Species open for freshwater fish claims (Minimum qualifying weights) — **Silver Bream** (1 lb). Qualifying weights are subject to revision by the Committee if necessary.

● *The Editor wishes to thank Mr Peter Tombleson and the British Record (rod caught) Fish Committee for their assistance in compiling these lists.*

SEA FISH (Shore records)

	Weight lb oz dr	kilogrms	Captor and Venue	Date
Angler Fish	68 2 0:	30 899	H. G. T. Legerton, Canvey Island, Essex	1967
Bass	18 2 0:	8 220	F. C. Borley, Felixstowe, Suffolk	1943
Black-fish	1 0 0:	0 454	Qualifying weight	—
Bluemouth	1 0 0:	0 454	Qualifying weight	—
Bogue	1 15 4:	0 885	S. G. Torode, Pembroke, Guernsey, C.I.	1978
Bream, Black	4 14 12:	2 232	D. P. Bohan, Alderney, C.I.	1984
Bream, Gilthead	8 2 2:	3 688	A. Marquand, Guernsey, C.I.	1983
Bream, Ray's	7 15 12:	3 621	G. Walker, Crimdon Beach, Hartlepool	1967
Bream, Red	4 7 0:	2 012	A. Salmon, Alderney, C.I.	1979
Brill	7 7 8:	3 387	B. M. K. Fletcher, Guernsey, C.I.	1980
Bull Huss	17 15 0:	8 136	M. Roberts, Falmouth, Cornwall	1977
Catfish	12 12 8:	5 797	G. M. Taylor, Stonehaven, Scotland	1978
Coalfish	20 6 0:	9 214	D. Cook, Newquay, Cornwall	1982
Cod	44 8 0:	20 183	B. Jones, Toms Points, Barry, Glam.	1966
Comber	0 12 0:	0 340	Qualifying weight	—
Common Skate	100 0 0:	45 357	Qualifying weight	—
Conger	67 1 0:	30 417	A. W. Lander, Arch Rock End, Torquay	1967
Dab	2 9 8:	1 176	M. L. Watts, Port Talbot, Wales	1936
Dogfish, Black-Mouthed	0 12 0:	0 340:	Qualifying weight	—
Dogfish, Lesser Spotted	4 8 0:	2 040	J. Beattie, off Ayr Pier, Scotland	1969
Flounder	5 2 0:	2 324	W. Stevens, Teign Estuary, Devon	1978

Alan Wilson, who is a Blackpool specimen hunter, boosted the British tench record by 2½lb. with this 12lb. 8oz. 11dms. heavyweight, caught in Wilstone Reservoir, Hertfordshire, where the previous record tench of 10lb. 1¼oz. was taken in 1981.

The shore-caught national national record for pollack, last broken in 1977, fell to Derek Litten, of Preston, Dorset, for this 18lb. 2oz. beauty landed at Chesil Beach. The 1977 record of 16lb. came from the next beach along, at Portland Bill

Sea fish (Shore records) *continued*

	Weight lb	oz	dr	kilogrms	Captor and Venue	Date
Forkbeard. Greater	1	0	0:	0 454	Qualifying weight	—
Garfish	2	15	9:	1 347	M. Wills, Coverack, Cornwall	1979
Greater Weever	1	7	8:	0 666	D. C. Charman, nr. Porthcurno, Cornwall	1983
Gurnard, Grey	1	8	0:	0 680	S. Quine, Isle of Man	1977
Gurnard, Red	2	10	11:	1 209	D. Johns, Helford River, Cornwall	1976
Gurnard, Streaked	1	6	8:	0 637	H. Livingstone Smith, Loch Goil, Firth of Clyde	1971
Gurnard, Yellow or Tubfish	12	3	0:	5 528	G. J. Reynolds, Langland Bay, Wales	1976
Haddock	6	12	0:	3 061	G. B. Stevenson, Loch Goil, Firth of Clyde	1976
Haddock, Norway	1	3	0:	0 538	F. P. Fawke, Southend Pier, Essex	1973
Hake	3	8	2:	1 590	W. S. Parry, Morfa Beach, Glamorgan	1984
Halibut	10	0	0:	4 536	Qualifying weight	—
Herring	1	0	0:	4 454	Qualifying weight	—
John Dory	3	0	0:	1 361	Qualifying weight	—
Ling	19	4	0:	8 731	D. J. Rogan, SW coast of Jersey, C.I.	1981
Lumpsucker	14	3	0:	6 435	W. J. Burgess, off Felixstowe Beach, Suffolk	1970
Mackerel	5	11	14:	2 603	M. A. Kemp, Berry Head Quarry, Brixham	1982
Megrim	1	11	11:	0 784	N. A. Morse, Porth Chapel, nr Penzance	1984
Monkfish	52	14	0:	23 982	G. S. Bishop, Llwyngwril Beach, N. Wales	1984
Mullet, Golden Grey	2	10	4:	1 197	F. Odire, Alderney, C.I.	1983
Mullet, Red	3	10	0:	1 644	J. E. Martell, Guernsey, C.I.	1967
Mullet, Thick-Lipped Grey	14	2	12:	6 427	R. Gifford, Aberthaw, Glam.	1979
Mullet, Thin-Lipped Grey	6	4	0:	2 835	H. Mepham, River Rother, Sussex	1981
Opah	20	0	0:	9 071	Qualifying weight	—
Pelamid (Bonito)	2	0	0:	0 907	Qualifying weight	—
Perch, Dusky	7	0	0:	3 175	Qualifying weight	—
Plaice	8	1	4:	3 664	N. Mills, Southend Pier, Essex	1976
Pollack	18	2	0:	8 220	D. V. Litten, Chesil Beach, Dorset	1984
Pouting (Bib, Pout)	3	6	0:	1 580	W. Reid, Bossington Beach, Somerset	1983
Ray, Blonde	30	4	0:	13 720	J. T. Lowe, Nth. Coast, Jersey, C.I.	1980
Ray, Bottle-nosed	15	0	0:	6 804	Qualifying weight	—
Ray, Cuckoo	4	10	0:	2 097	C. Wills, North Cliffs, Cornwall	1981
Ray, Eagle	15	0	0:	6 804	Qualifying weight	—
Ray, Electric	52	11	0:	23 897	M. A. Wills, Porthallow, Cornwall	1980
Ray, Sandy	2	0	0:	0 907	Qualifying weight	—
Ray, Small-eyed	14	2	11:	6 426	A. Martinez, Trevose Head, Cornwall	1981
Ray, Spotted	8	5	0:	3 770	D. Bowen, Gower Peninsula, Wales	1980
Ray, Sting	51	4	0:	23 245	A. L. Stevens, Sowley Beach, Hants	1975
Ray, Thornback	21	6	0:	9 690	P. Paterson, Mull of Galloway, Scotland	1984
Ray, Undulate	21	4	0:	9 638	K. Skinner, Jersey, C.I.	1983
Rockling, 3-bearded	2	14	13:	1 328	F. A. Leason, Bempton Cliffs, Humberside	1984
Rockling, Shore	1	1	4:	0 488	A. Bayes, Gristhorpe, Scarborough	1976
Salmon, Coho	1	8	1:	0 681	R. J. McCracken, St. Sampsons, Guernsey, C.I.	1977
Sea-scorpion (Short-spined)	2	7	8:	1 119	B. Logan, Whitley Bay, Tyne & Wear	1982
Scad (Horse Mackerel)	3	0	14:	1 384	R. Dillon, Cockenzie, Scotland	1981
Shad, Allis	4	12	7:	2 166	P. Gerrard, Chesil Beach, Dorset	1977
Shad, Twaite	2	12	0:	1 247	J. W. Martin, Garlieston, Wigtownshire, Scotland	1978
Shark, Blue	40	0	0:	18 143	Qualifying weight	—

Sea fish (Shore records) *continued*

	Weight lb oz dr	kilogrms	Captor and Venue	Date
Shark, Mako	40 0 0:	18 143	Qualifying weight	—
Shark, Porbeagle	40 0 0:	18 143	Qualifying weight	—
Shark, Thresher	40 0 0:	18 143	Qualifying weight	—
Shark, six-gilled	5 2 0:	2 268	Qualifying weight	—
Smoothhound, Starry	23 2 0:	10 488	D. Carpenter, Beach, Bradwell-on-Sea, Essex	1972
Smoothhound	15 12 12:	7 165	G. E. Jones, Boverston, Glam.	1981
Sole	6 1 14:	2 773	J. Bartram, Alderney, C.I.	1984
Sole, Lemon	2 7 11:	1 124	W. N. Callister, Douglas, I.O.M.	1980
Spanish Mackerel	0 12 0:	0 340	Qualifying weight	—
Spurdog	16 12 8:	7 611	R. Legg, Chesil Beach, Dorset	1964
Sunfish	49 4 0:	22 338	M. Merry, North Cliffs, Cornwall	1976
Tadpole Fish	1 3 12:	0 559	D. Higgins, Whitley Bay, Tyne & Wear	1977
Tope	58 2 0:	26 363	R. J. White, Baggy Point, North Devon	1982
Torsk	3 0 0:	1 361	Qualifying weight	—
Trigger Fish	4 6 0:	1 984	M. J. Blew, Bossington Beach, Somerset	1975
Tunny	40 0 0:	18 143	Qualifying weight	—
Turbot	28 8 0:	12 926	J. D. Dorling, Dunwich Beach, Suffolk	1973
Whiting	4 0 7:	1 826	T. Dell, Chesil Beach, Dorset	1984
Whiting, Blue (Poutassou)	0 12 0:	0 340	Qualifying weight	—
Witch	1 2 13:	0 533	T. J. Barathy, Colwyn Bay, N. Wales	1967
Wrasse, Ballan	8 6 6:	3 808	R. W. LePage, Bordeaux Beach, Guernsey, C.I.	1976
Wrasse, Cuckoo	1 12 1:	0 796	A. J. Smart, Alderney, C.I.	1984
Wreck Fish	1 0 0:	0 454	Qualifying weight	—

SEA FISH (Boat records)

	Weight lb oz dr	kilogrms	Captor and Venue	Date
Angler Fish	82 12 0:	37 533	K. Ponsford, Mevagissey, Cornwall	1977
Bass	18 6 0:	8 334	R. G. Slater, off Eddystone Reef, Plymouth	1975
Black-fish	3 10 8:	1 658	James Semple, off Head of Ayr, Scotland	1972
Bluemouth	3 2 8:	1 431	Anne Lyngholm, Loch Shell, Stornoway	1976
Bogue	1 13 0:	0 822	K. McBride, Eddystone Reef	1981
Bream, Black	6 14 4:	3 125	J. Garlick (Torquay), wreck off Devon coast	1977
Bream, Gilthead	5 3 4:	2 360	P. King, Salcombe, Devon	1983
Bream, Ray's	6 3 13:	2 829	J. Holland, Barra Head, Scotland	1978
Bream, Red	9 8 12:	4 330	B. H. Reynolds, off Mevagissey, Cornwall	1974
Brill	16 0 0:	7 257	A. H. Fisher, Isle of Man	1950
Bull Huss	21 3 0:	9 610	J. Holmes, Looe, Cornwall	1955
Catfish	24 3 0:	10 971	N. Trevelyan, Whitby, Yorks.	1980
Coalfish	35 14 0:	15 988	T. Neatby, off Whitby, Yorks.	1983
Cod	53 0 0:	24 039	G. Martin, Start Point, Devon	1972
Comber	1 13 0:	0 822	B. Phillips, Mounts Bay, Cornwall	1977
Common Skate	226 8 0:	102 733	R. S. Macpherson, Duny Voe, Shetland	1970
Conger	109 6 0:	49 609	R. W. Potter, S. E. of Eddystone, Plymouth	1976
Dab	2 12 4:	1 254	R. Islip, Gairloch, Wester Ross, Scotland	1975
Dogfish, Black-Mouthed	2 13 8:	1 288	J. H. Anderson, Loch Fyne, Scotland	1977
Dogfish, Lesser Spotted	4 1 13:	1 865	B. J. Solomon, Newquay, Cornwall	1976
Flounder	5 11 8:	2 593	A. G. L. Cobbledick, Fowey, Cornwall	1956
Forkbeard, Greater	4 11 4:	2 133	Miss M. Woodgate, Falmouth Bay, Cornwall	1969
Garfish	3 0 2:	1 363	J. Nardini, Penzance	1981
Greater Weever	2 4 0:	1 020	P. Ainslie, Brighton	1927
Gurnard, Grey	2 7 0:	1 105	D. Swinbanks, Caliach Point, Mull, Scotland	1976
Gurnard, Red	5 0 0:	2 268	B. D. Critchley. off Rhyl, Wales	1973
Gurnard, Streaked	0 12 0:	0 340	Qualifying weight	—
Gurnard, Yellow or Tubfish	11 7 4:	5 195	C. W. King, Wallasey, Cheshire	1952
Haddock	13 11 4:	6 215	G. Bones, off Falmouth, Cornwall	1978
Haddock, Norway	1 13 8:	0 836	T. Barrett, off Southend	1975
Hake	25 5 8:	11 494	H. W. Steele, Belfast Lough, Nth. Ireland	1962
Halibut	234 0 0:	106 136	C. Booth, Dunnet Head, Thurso, Scotland	1979
Herring	1 1 0:	0 481	Brett Barden, off Bexhill, Sussex	1973
John Dory	11 14 0:	5 386	J. Johnson, Newhaven, Sussex	1977
Ling	57 8 0:	26 080	I. Duncan, off Stonehaven, Scotland	1982
Lumpsucker	10 12 0:	4 876	D. W. Jordan, off Shoreham, Sussex	1980
Mackerel	6 2 7:	2 790	W. J. Chapple, off Penberth Cove, Cornwall	1984
Megrim	3 12 8:	1 715	P. Christie, Loch Gairloch, Scotland	1973
Monkfish	66 0 0:	29 936	C. G. Chalk, Shoreham, Sussex	1965
Mullet, Golden Grey	1 14 4:	0 857	R. Smith, Falmouth, Cornwall	1981
Mullet, Red	3 7 0:	1 559	M. Hamel, Vale Guernsey, C. I.	1981
Mullet, Thick-Lipped Grey	10 1 0:	4 564	P. C. Libby, Portland, Dorset	1952
Mullet, Thin-Lipped Grey	3 7 0:	1 599	D. Davenport, Christchurch Estuary, Hants.	1983
Opah	128 0 0:	58 057	A. R. Blewett, Mounts Bay, Penzance	1973
Pelamid (Bonito)	8 13 4:	4 004	J. Parnell, Torbay, Devon	1969
Perch, Dusky	28 0 0:	12 700	D. Cope, off Durlston Head, Dorset	1973
Plaice	10 3 8:	4 635	H. Gardiner, Longa Sound, Scotland	1974

Sea fish (Boats) records *continued*

Pollack	26 7 0:	11 991	R. C. Perry, South of Salcombe, Devon	1984
Pouting (Bib, Pout)	5 8 0:	2 494	R. S. Armstrong, off Berry Head, Devon	1969
Ray, Blonde	37 12 0:	17 122	H. T. Pout, off Start Point, Devon	1973
Ray, Bottle-nosed	76 0 0:	34 471	R. Bulpitt, off Needles, Isle of Wight	1970
Ray, Cuckoo	5 11 0:	2 579	V. Morrison, off Causeway Coast, N.I.	1975
Ray, Eagle	52 8 0:	23 812	R. J. Smith, off Nab Tower, Isle of Wight	1972
Ray, Electric	96 1 0:	43 571	N. J. Cowley, off Dodman Point, Cornwall	1975
Ray, Marbled Electric	2 8 8:	1 148	B. T. Maguire, Jersey, C.I.	1983
Ray, Sandy	2 0 0:	0 907	Qualifying weight	—
Ray, Small-eyed	16 6 8:	7 441	J. Lush, off Minehead, Somerset	1982
Ray, Spotted	7 12 0:	3 515	J. Cochrane, Causeway Coast, N.I.	1982
Ray, Sting	61 8 0:	27 894	V. W. Roberts, Pwllheli, Gwynedd	1979
Ray, Thornback	38 0 0:	17 236	J. Patterson, Rustington, Sussex	1935
Ray, Undulate	20 12 4:	9 418	F. J. Casado, Corbiere, Jersey, C.I.	1982
Rockling, 3-bearded	3 2 0:	1 417	N. Docksey, Portland Breakwater, Dorset	1976
Rockling, Shore	0 12 0:	0 340	Qualifying weight	—
Salmon, Coho	1 0 0:	0 454	Qualifying weight	—
Sea-scorpion (Short-spined)	2 3 0:	0 992	R. Stephenson, Gt. Cumrae Island, Scotland	1976
Scad (Horse Mackerel)	3 5 3:	1 507	M. A. Atkins, Torbay, Devon	1978
Shad, Allis	2 0 0:	0 907	Qualifying weight	—
Shad, Twaite	(3 2 0:	1 417)	T. Hayward, Deal	1949
	(3 2 0:	1 417)	S. Jenkins, Torbay	1954
Shark, Blue	218 0 0:	98 878	N. Sutcliffe, Looe, Cornwall	1959
Shark, Mako	500 0 0:	226 786	Mrs J. M. Yallop, off Eddystone, Devon	1971
Shark, Porbeagle	465 0 0:	210 910	J. Potier, off Padstow, Cornwall	1976
Shark, Thresher	323 0 0:	146 504	S. Mills, Nab Tower, Portsmouth	1982
Shark, six-gilled	9 8 0:	4 309	F. E. Beeton, Penlee Point, Plymouth	1976
Smoothhound, Starry	28 0 0:	12 700	R. Grady, Maplin Sands, Essex	1980
Smoothhound	28 0 0:	12 700	A. T. Chivers, Heacham, Norfolk	1969
Sole	3 12 4:	1 708	S. Brice, Fishbourn Creek, IoW	1980
Sole, Lemon	2 2 0:	0 963	J. Gordon, Loch Goil Head, Scotland	1976
Spanish Mackerel	1 0 6:	0 464	P. Jones, off Guernsey, C.I.	1972
Spurdog	21 3 7:	9 622	P. Barrett, Porthleven, Cornwall	1977
Sunfish	108 0 0:	48 986	T. F. Sisson, Saundersfoot, Pembs., Wales	1976
Tadpole Fish	0 15 2:	0 428	N. G. Davies, Milford Haven, Dyfed	1976
Tope	74 11 0:	33 876	A. S. Harris, Caldy Island, Dyfed	1964
Torsk	15 7 2:	7 005	D. J. Mackay, Pentland Firth, Scotland	1982
Trigger Fish	4 9 5:	2 077	E. Montacute, Weymouth Bay	1975
Tunny	851 0 0:	385 989	L. Mitchell Henry, Whitby, Yorks	1933
Turbot	33 12 0:	15 308	R. Simcox, Kingsbridge, Devon	1980
Whiting	6 12 0:	3 061	N. R. Croft, Falmouth, Cornwall	1981
Whiting, Blue (Poutassou)	1 12 0:	0 793	J. H. Anderson, Loch Fyne, Scotland	1977
Witch	0 12 0:	0 340	Qualifying weight	—
Wrasse, Ballan	9 6 0:	4 252	M. Goodacre, Eddystone Gully	1981
Wrasse, Cuckoo	2 0 8:	0 921	A. M. Foley, off Plymouth	1973
Wreck Fish	10 10 0:	4 819	B. McNamara, off Eddystone Reef	1980

HOW TO CLAIM

● KEEP THE FISH in its natural state, dead or alive, for inspection by someone appointed by the Records Committee. In most instances it should not be necessary to kill freshwater coarse fish as a Committee representative can normally inspect in a matter of hours.

● TELEPHONE the Committee Secretary (telephone numbers and address shown below) for advice on procedure, preservation and identification.

● SEND a written claim as follow-up, stating species, weight, date and place of capture, tackle used, shore or boat fishing for sea fish PLUS names and addresses of reliable witnesses to the capture and weight as they will be asked to sign forms supporting the claims. DON'T LET WITNESSES GET AWAY!

● IF you are caught without witnesses, be prepared to swear an affidavit in support of the claim so keep all the details for this.

● RECORDS make news and Angler's Mail weekly is there to present it. So the next 'phone call is to Angler's Mail Newsdesk, reversing the charges (telephone numbers printed on Page Two of Angler's Mail every week). Reporters will want to know if pictures are available or can be taken by a local cameraman. You can also check with them on the latest official records.

● THE Secretary of the British Record (rod-caught) Fish Committee is Mr Peter Tombleson, National Anglers' Council, 11 Cowgate, Peterborough PE1 1LZ. Telephone (day) Peterborough (0733) 54084 or (evenings) 252428.

JOHN INGHAM

Bill Chapple, from St. Buryan, Cornwall, hooked this monster mackerel of 6lb. 2oz, while boat fishing off Pemberth and smashed a national record which had stood since 1969.

We asked some of Britain's best-known specialist anglers to choose the six venues that have become their personal favourites over the years. Their response is a fascinating blend of childhood memories, a deep love of the countryside and awareness of their surroundings — plus, of course, an affection for those waters that helped build their angling reputations.

MY FAVOURI

BAILEY ON ROACH

WENSUM

I SUPPOSE I must start with the Wensum, the gentle river that meanders through farmland from Fakenham to the heart of Norwich in Norfolk, before losing its identity with the Yare. No roach water has been so kind to me over the years since I landed my first big fish there back in the 1960s.

During the mid-70s, it yielded score upon score of 2lb fish for me and my friends, including dozens over 2¾lb. I was lucky enough to land two three-pounders in this period and I lost a fish nearer 4lb on one cold February night. But the icing on the cake came in the autumn of 1985 when, after many blank sessions, I landed my biggest roach to date and a record for the county at 3lb 10oz. That fish was one of a handful of survivors from the plentiful days.

There is much more to Wensum roach fishing than the sheer size of the fish. The beauty of the valley has always meant just as much to me. I love its stark loneliness, its sombre colours and the way the wind dies at dusk as the duck flight in. So, that's why I still fish there every winter, though the rewards, in terms of numbers, are not as great as they were ten years ago. But the chance of a fish of record size still exists.

Not only are there less fish but there is also less accessible bank than there used to be. Much is private or owned by syndicates and there are few stretches where the general angling public can fish on a day ticket.

Thus, in these ways, the Wensum is not quite the great river of freedom it once was, but I will never leave it.

BURE

FOR me, roach fishing on the Bure means the Upper Bure, along the river that runs upstream of Horstead Mill towards Aylsham, Norfolk. But it is impossible to name

JOHN BAILEY, who is a Norfolk schoolteacher, must rank as Britain's top roach angler with a record that speaks for itself: three roach over 3lb., hundreds over 2lb. in recent seasons and an understanding of the species that few can equal. His six favouite hunting grounds reflect his genuine and deep love of the countryside as much as his fondness for fishing.

John Bailey with a superb 2¾lb roach from his favourite venue, the River Wensum in Norfolk.

favoured stretches as the few roach shoals are immensely mobile from season to season.

I tend to wander miles after them, hoping to spot fish on the surface and trotting long distances with large pieces of flake that might produce an instant take and lead me on to a concetration of roach.

I find the Bure valley nowhere near as appealing as the Wensum's but I constantly return to what is an even greater challenge with the possibility of even larger fish. Bure fish — bream as well as roach — have historically had a slightly higher ceiling weight and I have always believed that a 3½ pounder is a possibility. Such a fish would be the high spot of any roach man's career.

My close friend, John Nunn, came so close to such a fish with a fabulous 3lb. 3oz. roach a couple of winters ago.

WAVENEY

This completes my trio of Norfolk rivers and, in many ways, is quite different to either the Bure or the Wensum. The majority of the fish do not run nearly so big and, indeed, my best roach there is 2lb. 9oz. which is quite moderate by Wensum standards.

Secondly, there are more fish in the Waveney. On my favourite areas around Earsham Mill or Bungay it is possible to find swims that will yield numbers of roach, rather than the odd solitary fish of the waters farther north.

I also like the intimacy of the Waveney's sharp bends, alder-hung pools and slow weedy slacks. It is a river that reminds me much of my roach fishing nursery on the River Dane in Cheshire.

The same methods work as well: close in stret-pegging; floating caster on the top at dusk; tight, short trotting on light gear and legering with a bomb tiny enough to move in the current and search the areas on the far bank.

ARDLEIGH RESERVOIR

EACH autumn I look forward to my roaching trips to this marvellous trout water where, sensibly, the doors are opened for coarse fishing at the end of the fly season.

For some reason, I like the feel of the place. I love to see the wind whip it to a maelstrom and I admire the ever-changing skies there, bringing sun and rain in quick succession during this changeable season. The banks are big enough to escape the crowds and the changing shoreline allows endless experiments in differing water levels on both float and lead.

I have always enjoyed big still-water roach fishing since my early days on Rudyard and Poynton Pool but here the rewards are greater both in size and numbers. Over the years, my fishing has become more and more specialised and I relish the chance, once or twice a year to "bag up", to really put together a big net of fish. I suppose it is the "blood lust" in me that is generally kept well under control, but is allowed free rein at Ardleigh.

I have also always felt that a very big roach is a possibility at the reservoir. My best have only scraped 2lb so far, but I still believe better are to come.

TWEED

WHENEVER we can afford it, Sharon and I book a week's salmon fishing on the River Tweed. When the fresh, silver giants are running, nothing could be more stimulating — but life's ironies generally ensure that our weeks coincide with low water and stale, red fish.

Then, there is the choice of either persevering in the salmon boats, knowing that valuable holiday time is being wasted or setting out to explore with light fly gear for trout or with coarse tackle for roach. But it is for the roach that I generally turn.

Tweed roach have a certain magic that perhaps only those who have fished for them will know. They always seem deeper and more vividly coloured to me than my English fish. They fight well, too, pulling normal roach gear to the limit when they reach a strong current.

Finding Tweed roach is always the vital problem. The shoals appear to be highly mobile and, of course, they are perpetually harassed by the netsmen who want them out of a game river. I have always concentrated on the great areas of slack water that dot this magnificent river and I have contacted fish from Kelso to Coldstream, to Norham and even farther down river under the iron bridge at Horncliffe.

Part of the glory of Tweed roaching for me is the exploration of the river. I have got to know many, many miles of the lovely lower valley and I can close my eyes now and see a dozen swims that have given marvellous sport.

CORK BLACKWATER

I HAVE fished this legendary southern Irish river for roach only on isolated occasions but in each session there is an event I find impossible ever to forget.

I fished the notorious bacon factory at Cappoquin before its closure, using for bait the congealed blood that fell through the waste pipes into the river and caught near 2lb roach on lumps large enough to cover a size 6 hook.

I was covered in brine and my Barbour jacket smelt of the slaughter near two years after. By the end of a day there I would be sickened by the stench and deafened by the cries of the dying animals and yet each time I would drive away knowing that I would soon return.

Out of the town, I have spent days in the wilds of the mild soft, countryside, wandering, exploring, fishing swims that might never have seen a roach angler before.

The rewards have always been fabulous: large dace, brown trout, sea trout, once a salmon chasing a feeder and, above all, glorious roach averaging one to 1½lb. It has mostly been raining on me — that's Ireland!— but you tend to forgive and forget as the fish come steadily to the net and only the sighing forests look down on you.

ORME ON CHUB

Andy Orme chub-spotting near the famous School Bridge at Throop, on the Dorset Stour.

ANDY ORME is a dedicated speciment hunter from Marlborough, in Wiltshire, and has caught thousands of chub, including some very fine fish, from scores of different venues. But here he narrows his personal favourites to just six.

THROOP FISHERY

THROOP is one of the most consistent chub fisheries on the Dorset Stour. I have spent hundreds of happy days wandering its banks and I served my "chubber's" apprenticeship there.

Back in the late 1960s, stalking the river with lumps of cheese and crust, I learned the importance of concealment and careful observation. Those that blundered about caught nothing.

It was also at Throop that I learned the value of natural baits. A day with cheese produced a few good fish but great fat orange slugs produced a dozen and the bites almost took the rod out of my hand!

What makes Throop such a lovely chub water is the nature of the river. There are dozens of quite shallow swims where chunky chub can be watched for hours but they are no mugs. These days they see plenty of baits and so you have got either to offer them something novel or present a conventional bait very effectively.

All in all, some of the happiest days of my life have been spent at Throop. I have met some great people there some of whom have remained my closest friends.

DORSET STOUR

THE Longham stretch of the Dorset Stour offers scope for stalking and also possesses some great trotting swims. Like Throop I've fished here for years and consistently caught good chub.

I love catching fish on the float and at Longham you can trot flake among a trail of mashed bread and land chub after chub. One of my burning ambitions is to land a 6lb chub from a river and I would like to get it trotting. I would not be at all surprised that if I do get a "6" it will come from this stretch of the Stour.

Unfortunately, I have a suspicion that if such a specimen is lurking there it will take more than a bit of bread to fool it. Trouble is, trotting with flake is just so enjoyable that I can't stop doing it!

HAMPSHIRE AVON

IT took me years to catch a 5lb chub. I finally did it on the Hampshire Avon and the Royalty Fishery was the venue. Not surprisingly, I therefore include it in my list of favourite chub stretches.

When I cracked the "5" barrier I was living in Exeter, which is about 80 miles from Christchurch. I also had a full-time job as a freshwater biologist and

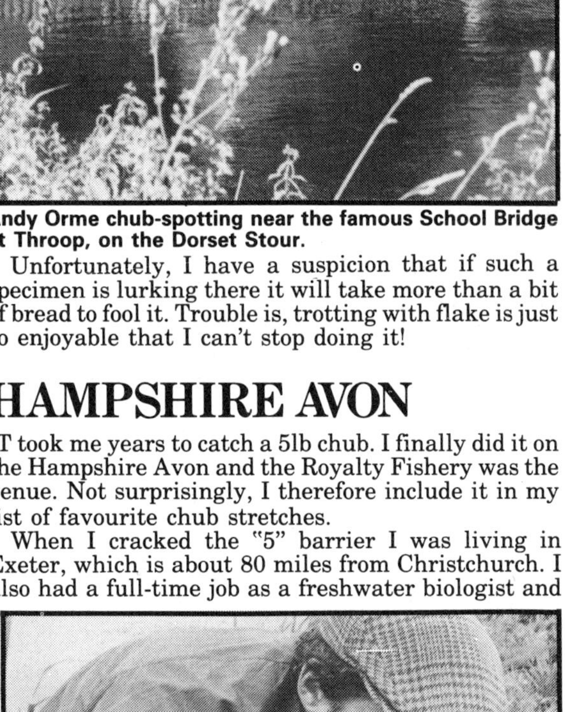

This lovely 4lb-plus chub came from the Bat and Ball stretch of the Hampshire Avon, one of Andy's favourite waters.

to get a mid-week evening session took a lot of effort. I drove a clapped-out old A40 at breakneck speeds and used to run to my swim.

The actual spot where I landed my first "5" is one of the most pretty I know. Beautiful willows trail over a clean gravel run, wild mint exudes a refreshing fragrance and, in those days, very big chub could be spotted occasionally.

Touch-legering and striking at tiny twitch bites produced the fish and I can remember that chub as clearly as if I had caught it yesterday.

Sadly, the Royalty is now a shadow of its former self and the prices for tickets do not, I feel represent value for money.

Another particularly lovely reach of the Hampshire Avon with a good head of chub and a fine pub up the road as well, is the Bat and Ball stretch at Fordingbridge.

The mill stream used to offer great chubbing until it had the heart dredged out of it. Now it is only the main river where I get the fish unless they are forced into the stream by heavy flooding.

Although I know of six-pounders being taken here in the past a 5lb chub is probably top whack these days. But no matter, on a good day I can take several fish and in the late autumn and winter months trotting bread is a killing method. Trotting maggots is also very productive but because the chub have seen it all before I sometimes have to resort to size 20 hooks and very light lines.

RIVER KENNET

I SPENT quite a while at the University of Reading, studying freshwater biology and this meant I was ideally situated to exploit one of Britain's finest rivers.

Although the River Kennet flows through some lovely countryside I used to fish the Reading free town centre stretch a lot. But this was not without its dangers! When chubbing opposite the Courage Brewery I was in full view of people piling out of various pubs and a right load of abuse used to be hurled in my direction by some very dubious-looking characters.

I managed to survive the aggro, though, and caught some big fish to almost 5lb. They were very finicky chub and bites were almost impossible to detect. No matter what bait I tried all I would get was a slight tightening of the line as a chub mouthed the bait and that would be my lot. I reckon I hit one bite in ten.

RIVER NENE

I HAVE only ever caught one chub from the River Nene at Oundle in Northamptonshire and it weighed only 2lb 4oz. Mind you, I was only about 12 at the time and so it seemed absolutely huge to my young eyes.

My old mate, Phil Blades, lived in a pub called the Wheatsheaf Inn at Upper Benefield and in the school holidays I got the train to Northants and we spent many happy days catching all sorts of fish from the Nene.

On the day I caught my 2lb chub we had spent some time gathering big marshworms from under decaying reed mats washed up by recent flood waters. I stuck one on a crude leger rig and hurled it into the tail of the weir pool expecting a perch. The rod was placed in a couple of rests and I did just about anything other than sit by it waiting for a bite.

Luckily, when I did get a take I was only about 30ft from the rod and the chub obligingly hung on for ages. My young legs trembled as I wound that fish in and when it was on the bank I was beside myself with glee.

That is a very dear memory to me and so deserves a place in this list.

SIDLEY ON EELS

JOHN SIDLEY, of Birmingham, has been eel-fishing since he was six years old and now has 104 over 4lb to his credit with a personal best of 8lb 3oz, which is a mighty eel by any reckoning. John's interest in eels is so strong that he has founded a "Put Eels Back" campaign and he has written several books about them. This is his choice of favourite eel grounds.

John Sidley with one of many large eels he has landed at a variety of different venues.

EARLSWOOD LAKES, WARWICKSHIRE

MY first thoughts about favourite venues always turn to a small lake at the Earlswood complex, known locally as the "private lake." This was the first stillwater I ever fished for eels and over the years it has been very good to me, producing my personal best of 8lb 3oz, two over 7lb, six over 6lb and many over 5lb, with the majority taken on legered lobworms, which, in my book, is the best bait for eels.

Not an expensive water to fish, costing just £1.40 a day; night-fishing is banned which, I'm sure, prevents even bigger eels from being taken. The private lake also produced my first-ever pike over 20lb, a lovely 25lb specimen and, later, I went on to land a 28¼lb-pounder which still holds the lake record.

So you can see I have very special reasons for voting this water top of my personal charts.

Continued overleaf

MY FAVOURITE WATERS

WESTWOOD PARK, DROITWICH, WORCS.

THIS is another of my all-time favourites and the scene of some of my best and biggest catches. I once devoted all my free time to fishing this water, putting in a stint that lasted over 12 weeks non-stop. It got to the stage where my wife was thinking of re-addressing my mail to the "bivvy" on the end of the dam wall — such was the fascination I had for this water.

My best catch from Westwood was one of 23 eels weighing over 68lb, including three over 4lb, which I think, is some kind of record. My heaviest from the lake weighed 7lb 14oz, which is still my second-largest eel. I caught the majority of my fish on four lobworms on a big hook, legered at long range, particularly at night.

This water also holds big roach and one angler landed a 4½lb roach on lobworms intended for eels, only to return it without claiming the British record.

RIVER SEVERN

THE lower reaches of the River Severn hold some excellent eels which will take any number of baits from casters to deadbaits, though the latter sort out better-class specimens.

My favourite spot is at Tewkesbury, around the Lower Loade Hotel, where day tickets cost £1 for excellent value. My best eel here weighed 4lb 11oz and fell to a dead bleak.

Farther upstream, the Birmingham AA stretch at Severn Stoke produced my best Severn eel, a 5½-pounder which took a lump of cheese — not one of my usual eel baits!

Another area on the Severn for good eels in the past is at Claines, just above Worcester, where the River Salwarpe flows into the Severn. I have had some fair bags of fish to around the 4lb mark on legered bleak deadbaits from this BAA-owned fishery.

COSGROVE LODGE PARK, NORTHAMPTON

I FIRST read about this water in an *Angler's Mail* "Where To Fish" article and since that time it has brought me specimens to nearly 6lb.

MARSDEN ON BREAM

GRAHAM MARSDEN, the famous Cheshire specimen hunter, is acknowledged as one of Britain's leading big bream specialists with an enviable list of personal heavyweights. His list of six favourite waters includes some that reflect the passing years and others he is currently fishing — but all have the potential for big bream.

Graham Marsden bends into a big bream at Mere Park, in Cheshire, which is his current favourite.

OULTON PARK LAKE, Cheshire

THIS lake gave me my first big catches of bream in the 2lb to 4lb class and for that reason it will always remain one of my favourite waters.

Fifty pounds of medium-sized bream may not seem much these days, but more than 20 years ago they were good enough to make headlines in the angling Press.

One of the nicest things about Oulton Park was its excellent winter sport for bream. I remember many occasions when we found the water partly covered with ice, but still managed to catch a dozen fish.

We used to "fill in" the swim with mashed bread and pig meal and fish with huge pieces of flake on No. 6 hooks. A large lump of flake was used as a dough-bobbin and most times the bream slammed it up to the butt ring with an audible slap.

No wonder we sometimes long for the "good old days"!

QUOISLEY MERE, Cheshire.

A BEAUTIFUL little mere that you could fish for two shillings a day and the one that gave me my first 7lb, 8lb, and 9lb bream.

Until we built a stage to fish in comfort we had to perch on wobbling planks laid over treacherously swampy banks. At night it wasn't a lot of fun if you missed your footing and had to spend several hours covered in black gunge and smelling like a septic tank!

In those days, if I caught one bream of 8lb or more in a session lasting from Friday night to Sunday lunch I thought I'd done well.

In the early days at Quoisley the bream wanted only bread flake, but as more anglers tried maggots, it wasn't long before they ignored bread entirely in preference for maggots.

Sadly, the vast majority of Quoisley bream were killed several years ago when the water became de-oxygenated and I haven't fished there since.

CHURCH MERE, Cheshire.

THIS is another very beautiful mere which exudes a tangible atmosphere reeking of big fish. I have never mastered this water, to the point where I can catch bream consistently, and nor has anyone else, mainly because it holds so few.

Long before the T.C. pit and Oxford's Queensford Lagoon produced

Cosgrove Lodge Park comprises six gravel pits and a mile of the Great Ouse and after many blank stints on the pits I turned my attentions to the river.

To my surprise, on the first night I landed four eels over 3lb using four lobworms. The next night was even better with seven eels, the best 5lb 13oz.

Over a period of two years I caught 12 eels over 4lb from this stretch of river, the best 5lb 15oz. I tried deadbaits but all my fish came to four or five lobs.

While fishing for eels I also caught bream to 6lb, chub to 3½lb, plus several double-figure pike.

SWAN LAKE, HEREFORD

THIS is a private club lake on the Welsh borders which holds carp to nearly 30lb, large roach and perch which, I think, could well topple the British record.

It was at the invitation of a club member that I first fished the lake for eels but found it very hard going with innumerable blanks. A run a month was about the norm, which suggested that the eel stocks were very low. But the average size was high and there was even an outside chance of a double-figure fish.

On one occasion while using a wire trace I suffered a bite-off from an eel that felt much bigger than my 8lb 13oz personal best. On another, an eel over 9lb mark was netted from the lake in an operation to remove unwanted perch and tench.

My best eel to date from Swan Lake is 5lb and I've taken three others over 4lb, four lobworms again being the successful bait.

STRATFORD CANAL, STRATFORD-ON-AVON

I WILL always remember this water with affection for it was while fishing with my father for tench, when still a youngster, that I first hooked a large eel.

It weighed 2½lb and I remember having to use all my strength to pull it from the water. As it lay on the bank, all bronze and solid muscle, I remember my fascination with the sheer power it had displayed. An eel angler was born from that moment!

their giant bream, I had sighted a bream in Church Mere which I estimated at more than 16lb. I saw it on only one occasion and got within touching distance, when it was among a group of spawning bream. I shall never forget that awesome bulk as it casually glided away from my punt and disappeared into a lily bed.

The biggest bream Church Mere has produced to date was taken by Dave Ankers in 1976 and weighed 13¼lb. It was a record at that time and made the front cover of Angler's Mail.

I've taken fish to over 9lb from this water and planned the downfall of an 11½ pounder, and also caught a 7¼lb roach/bream hybrid. Although a double figure bream from here still eludes me I love fishing it for its mysterious aura, and the fact that no-one really knows its true potential.

RIVER SHANNON, Athlone, Eire.

I LIKE fishing the Shannon as it's the only river I fish for bream and they are easy to catch. It is tremendous fun for a holiday angler who wants the fishing to be as carefree and relaxing as possible.

I remember that when I first fished the Shannon, a number of years ago, my set-up was a simple paternoster with 6lb line, and a swingtip. I thought this was quite a crude set-up but soon changed my mind when the swingtip straightened out viciously and the rod tip began bending before I had a chance to pick up the rod.

The stretch I fish holds very good, hard-fighting bream averaging 7lb apiece and they love big lumps of flake on big hooks. A lot of fun if you don't take it too seriously, but can become boring in more than short doses.

HORSEMERE, Cheshire.

I CAUGHT my first double-figure bream from here at 11lb 1oz, and as this was the first water from which I took a bream of more than 5lb, it remains a special favourite.

When I first fished it in the mid-1960s I used pieces of flake as big as half-crowns on size 2 hooks. These flat pieces of flake were ideal for sinking slowly on to the thick carpet of algae that lay on the bottom.

In those early days we caught the fish at no more than 40 yards range, for it was at this distance we could see the bream rolling. For some reason the anglers who followed us on to the water decided to fish at greater distances, and eventually everyone was fishing at 70 yards and more.

When I caught my 11-pounder in 1976 it took a couple of maggots on a No. 16 hook!

MERE PARK LAKE, Cheshire.

MY current favourite and where I'm conducting a number of experiments with bait and techniques.

Last season I took more than a hundred 8lb bream from here, with a best of 10lb 2oz. Most of these were taken on float tackle from a punt, using casters on small hooks and light line.

There were times when I had to go as fine as an 18 hook and 1.7lb line, though mostly I got away with a No. 16 to 2lb line. Fifty of those bream were taken in three incredible sessions, two of six hours duration and one of four hours, each beginning at 10am.

I've taken many guests to this water who have caught their best-ever bream and this always gives me a great deal of personal pleasure.

The mere lies in the very best of Cheshire countryside and even when I "blank", which is quite rare on this water, I can honestly say I still enjoy it.

A catch of 8lb-plus bream from one of Graham's favourite waters.

JOHN WATSON, from Sprowston, near Norwich, has a reputation second to none on his home waters in Norfolk, when it comes to catching big pike. But his No. 1 favourite water means a 1,000 mile round trip to Scotland's Loch Lomond. John explains why in this review of his favourite venues.

WATSON ON

ORMESBY-FILBY BROADS

SINCE moving to Norfolk in 1980 this group of Broads has become a firm favourite, providing pike in excess of 20lb to my rod every season. It is a popular complex but there is so much water — over 800 acres — that it is never crowded and I can always find ample areas away from other anglers.

This is a definite advantage, for competing against the fish is hard enough at times, without having to compete against other anglers to catch them! What's more, the Broads are not connected to one of Norfolk's tidal waterways so the problem of holiday craft never arises.

A good population of pike exists throughout these waters with the best in the 27-28lb range. Rarely does a visit fail to see at least one pike in the boat while on some days, provided I can locate a pack of pike, sport can be hectic with 13 fish to $22\frac{1}{4}$lb, representing my best day's fishing.

Boats are readily available and always kept by their owners in very serviceable condition and available at a moderate charge for hire, from Alexanders on Little Ormesby or John Barnes on Great Ormesby/Filby.

TIDAL RIVER BURE

LIVING in an area of abundant pike waters like Norfolk the choice of water types is wide and the lure of moving water ranks highly in my preferences.

The tidal River Bure is generally regarded as sluggish but according to the height of tide and the further downstream into the tidal influences one ventures, it can build up quite a speedy run-off. This allows both live and deadbaits to be trotted beneath a float, giving access to many more pike than with a static presentation.

A variation on this approach, and my favourite method on this water, is to troll very slowly two livebaits from a boat, one set to fish the margins while the other covers mid-river.

A blank day is the exception rather than the rule and I have taken fish to just over 30lb in the past few years. A static approach, however, can pay dividends and it is this diversity of successful methods which attracts me to this venue.

Cruiser traffic can be troublesome at times but once winter sets in, this abates, although seldom ceases completely. Away from the main river, there are numerous dykes, boatyards and lagoons, which, in winter, attract food fish by the thousands, especially in the town areas of Wroxham and Horning. Knowing that an easy meal is there for the taking it isn't at all surprising that these areas form a haven for many pike!

LOCH LOMOND

SINCE my first visit to Loch Lomond in 1976 I have been in love with it and without doubt it is my favourite pike water. A visit these days means a 1,000-mile round trip but I still manage at least one a year.

The pike can be hard to locate but well worth the effort for when they do turn up, their fighting qualities and sheer beauty make their English brethren pale in comparison. Here is a real fish, a fighter par excellence. Hook into a Lomond pike and you know you have a battle on your hands.

Nowhere else have I fished where the splendour of the scenery is matched by that of the quarry, but Lomond is such a place and while it can be mean and moody it will always be magnificent.

No pike angler worth his salt should miss the opportunity to fish Lomond, which at 25 miles long by 5 miles across, offers truly a multitude of areas which have never seen a pike angler.

ROCKLAND BROAD

MY biggest pike from this 50-acre water scaled just over 17lb and consequently, no doubt, a few eyebrows may be raised by readers when they see that it's one of my favourites.

However, pike fishing to me represents many things — one of the least important being the actual weight of the pike I catch. Certainly, I like to catch big pike but I have no objections to catching small ones, especially the stamp of fish to be found here, which fight all the way to the boat.

Rarely have I encountered English pike that fight like Rockland fish which have true fighting qualities.

The Broad is unfishable from the banks and with no hire boats available, pressure from pike anglers isn't heavy. Furthermore, the fish aren't big enough to attract a lot of Norfolk pike anglers.

In the late Autumn months, the pike fight like demons and accept both dead and livebaits and lures on occasions.

Big bags can sometimes be amassed, with close on 200lb to my rod being one red-letter day.

With the majority of fish under double-figures what they lack in pounds and ounces, they make up in enthusiasm. A "double" is a good-sized fish, with anything in excess of 15lb a real specimen. A real fun water — and fun to me is what fishing is all about.

WOODBASTWICK DECOY BROAD

THIS water is controlled by Norwich and District AA and will always appear in my Top Five. A very difficult water, even on its best days, but it presents the kind of challenge I relish, especially when I seek a change from some of the easier waters that I fish.

A tough nut to crack but well worth the effort. It was from this water, at dusk on a mild February day in 1981 that I was fortunate enough to capture my first 30lb-plus pike, at $31\frac{3}{4}$lb.

Norfolk 30-pounders rarely